Journal of Prisoners on Prisons

... allowing our experiences and analysis to be added to the forum that will constitute public opinion could help halt the disastrous trend toward building more fortresses of fear which will become in the 21ˢᵗ century this generation's monuments to failure.

Jo-Ann Mayhew (1988)

Volume 23
Number 1
2014

JOURNAL OF PRISONERS ON PRISONS

EDITORIAL STAFF:

Editor-in-Chief:	Bob Gaucher	Issue Editor:	Justin Piché
Associate Editors:	Susan Nagelsen	Editorial Assistants:	Ashley Chen
	Charles Huckelbury		Sarah Fiander
Managing Editors:	Justin Piché	Prisoners' Struggles Editor:	Kevin Walby
	Mike Larsen	Book Review Editor:	Pat Derby

EDITORIAL BOARD:

Stacie Alarie	Aaron Doyle	MaDonna Maidment	Rose Ricciardelli
Bree Carlton	Maritza Felices-Luna	Katharina Maier	Jeffrey Ian Ross
Mielle Chandler	Sylvie Frigon	Joane Martel	Viviane Saleh-Hanna
Vicki Chartrand	Christine Gervais	Shadd Maruna	Judah Schept
Bell Gale Chevigny	Anne-Marie Grondin	Erin McCuaig	Renita Seabrook
Panagiota Chrisovergis	Kelly Hannah-Moffatt	Dawn Moore	Rashad Shabazz
Elizabeth Comack	Stacey Hannem	Melissa Munn	Lisa Smith
Howard Davidson	Jennifer Kilty	Mecke Nagel	Dale Spencer
Claire Delisle	Michael Lenza	Karen Raddon	Brian Chad Starks
Eugene Dey	Tara Lyons	Stephen C. Richards	Kelly Struthers Montford
			Matt Yeager

The *Journal of Prisoners on Prisons* publishes two volumes a year. Its purpose is to encourage research on a wide range of issues related to crime, justice, and punishment by current and former prisoners. Donations to the *JPP* are welcomed.

SUBMISSIONS:

Current and former prisoners are encouraged to submit original papers, collaborative essays, discussions transcribed from tape, book reviews, and photo or graphic essays that have not been published elsewhere. The *Journal* does not usually publish fiction or poetry. The *Journal* will publish articles in either French or English. Articles should be no longer than 20 pages typed and double-spaced or legibly handwritten. Electronic submissions are gratefully received. Writers may elect to write anonymously or under a pseudonym. For references cited in an article, the writer should attempt to provide the necessary bibliographic information. Refer to the references cited in this issue for examples. Submissions are reviewed by members of the Editorial Board. Selected articles are corrected for composition and returned to the authors for their approval before publication. Papers not selected are returned with editor's comments. Revised papers may be resubmitted. Please submit bibliographical and contact information, to be published alongside articles unless otherwise indicated.

SUBCRIPTIONS, SUBMISSIONS AND ALL OTHER CORRESPONDENCE:

Journal of Prisoners on Prisons
c/o Justin Piché, Assistant Professor
Department of Criminology, University of Ottawa
Ottawa, Ontario, Canada K1N 6N5

e-mail: jpp@uottawa.ca
website: www.jpp.org

SUBCRIPTION RATES FOR 2013:

	One Year	Two Years	Three Years
Prisoners	$15.00	$28.00	$40.00
Individuals	$30.00	$56.00	$80.00
Prison Libraries & Schools, Libraries & Institutions	$60.00	$110.00	$150.00

Subscriptions by mail are payable in Canadian or American dollars. In Canada, 5% HST must be added to all orders. We encourage subscription purchases online at http://www.press.uottawa.ca/JPP_subscription

INDIVIDUAL COPIES AND BACK ISSUES:

Each regular issue is $15 and each double-issue is $25 (Canadian dollars) + shipping costs. In Canada, 5% HST must be added to all orders. Back issues can be purchased from the University of Ottawa Press at www.press.uottawa.ca/subject/criminology. If interested in obtaining issues that are out of print, please contact the *JPP* directly. Further information regarding course orders and distribution can be obtained from the University of Toronto Press at:

University of Toronto Press Inc.
5201 Dufferin Street
Toronto, Ontario, Canada M3H 5T8

phone: 1-800-565-9523
fax: 1-800-221-9985
e-mail: utpbooks@utpress.utoronto.ca
website: www.utpress.utoronto.ca/utp_D1/home.htm

Co-published by the University of Ottawa Press and the *Journal of Prisoners on Prisons*.

ISSN 0838-164X
ISBN 978-0-7766-0946-1

In This Issue

COVER ART

EDITOR'S INTRODUCTION

Knowing Inside:
Contributions from Within/Beyond the Walls
Justin Piché

In a period where there are more than 10 million human beings warehoused in jails, prisons and penitentiaries across the world (Walmsley, 2013), it is surprising that much of what takes place behind the walls continues to be invisible and that research on the lived realities of incarceration remains relatively scarce (Reiter, 2014). If this invisibility maintained by corporate and state actors allows for "the moral legitimacy that underwrites mass complicity" in state repression to assert itself, than "[i]mages of human suffering and human fragility play a big role in creating... moments of delegitimation" (Simon, 2014). It is in these instances of visibility that radical change (e.g. the elimination of structures of mass violence like the militarized police brutality that has come to light in Ferguson, Missouri in the wake Michael Brown's death) becomes possible (ibid). Although this is certainly not assured in the face of the "penal machinery" that is in place in the United States (De Giorgi, 2014) and elsewhere. Seen in this light, a counter-visual ethnography that "rehabilitates our ocular vantages to see what is not there but which structures the present carceral moment by illuminating the invisible, excavating the underground, revealing the inscribed landscape, and raising the ephemeral ghoulish presence" is integral "to envision and presage a counter-carceral future" (Schept, 2014, p. 218).

Given their direct and sustained experience of state repression, prisoners should have a central role in creating these counter-inscriptions that "could help halt the disastrous tend toward building more fortresses of fear which will become in the 21st century this generation's monuments to failure" (Mayhew, 1988). A recent debate on how to do "prison research differently" – that is differently than doing ethnographic work inside carceral facilities as seemingly detached and unemotional scholars – has renewed discussions on how this can be done (see Jewkes, 2014). Convict Criminology – particularly in its autoethnographic form – whereby former prisoners turned academics integrate their carceral experiences into their research is one approach proposed (see Newbold *et al.*, 2014). Having academics and prisoners collaborate together in research teams is another (see Ross *et al.*, 2014). Encouraging the development of more ethnographic work conducted by prisoners, like the kind facilitated through the efforts of those involved in the *Journal of Prisoners on Prisons* (JPP), has also been suggested (see Piché *et al.*, 2014).

In this issue of the *JPP*, readers will find these three kinds of contributions that, although in written form, offer alternative images that make visible that which takes place inside otherwise opaque prisons. In "From the Depths I Will Rise: On Being Buried Alive and Survival", Anonymous' prisoner ethnography recounts the violence of solitary confinement and how he survived the isolation. From there, Michael Johnson Jr. provides an autoethnographic account informed by Convict Criminology entitled "Institutionalized Indifference: Rape with a View", which explores the sexual violence that takes place in carceral facilities. Research team Robert "Diesel" Shoemaker, Brandon "B" Willis and Angela Bryant then explain how the Inside-Out Prison Exchange Program offers a way to counter the austerity and brutality of imprisonment in "We Are the Products of Our Experiences: The Role Higher Education Plays in Prisons". Offering another example of the team research approach, Daniel Luff and Greg Newbold discuss the pitfalls of risk management and prediction in "Risk Assessment in New Zealand Prisons: Questioning Experiential Outcomes". The article section concludes with a paper entitled "Seeing Shame: Prison Work and the Problem of Self-exclusion" by Alan Mobley that reflects upon the enduring consequences that incarceration has on the lives of former prisoners. Following a *Response* by *JPP* Editorial Board member Kevin Walby, the issue concludes with a prisoners' struggles piece by the John Howard Society of Ontario that explores their penal reform efforts in their near century of existence.

Book-ended by the art of Ronnie Goodman, this volume is the first issue of the *JPP* that will be fully available online as a free download on our website www.jpp.org. While readers are encouraged to continue purchasing subscriptions and hard copies of the journal where possible as sales sustain the publication, we encourage everyone to read and circulate the articles posted online widely. Perhaps when confronted by the images of penality offered in these pieces more conversations about how to think about and respond to violence in all of its forms will bloom, fostering transformative change (Morris, 2000) rather than more of the same (Cohen, 1985).

REFERENCES

Cohen, Stanley (1985) *Visions of Social Control*, Cambridge: Polity Press.

De Giorgi, Alessandro (2014) "Ferguson and Beyond: "Justifiable Homicides" and Premature Death in the Urban Ghetto", *Social Justice Blog* – August 21. Retrieved from: <http://www.socialjusticejournal.org/?p=2455>.

Jewkes, Yvonne (2014) "An Introduction to "Doing Prison Research Differently"", *Qualitative Inquiry*, 20(4): 387-391.

Mayhew, Joanne (1988) "Untitled", *Journal of Prisoners on Prisons*, 1(1): i.

Morris, Ruth (2000) *Stories of Transformative Justice*, Toronto: CSPI.

Newbold, Greg, Jeffrey Ian Ross, Richard S. Jones, Stephen C. Richards and Michael Lenza (2014) "Prison Research From the Inside: The Role of Convict Autoethnography", *Qualitative Inquiry*, 20(4): 454-463.

Piché, Justin, Bob Gaucher and Kevin Walby (2014) "Facilitating Prisoner Ethnography: An Alternative Approach to "Doing Prison Research Differently"", *Qualitative Inquiry*, 20(4): 392-403.

Reiter, Keramet (2014) "Making Windows in Walls: Strategies for Prison Research", *Qualitative Inquiry*, 20(4): 417-428.

Ross, Jeffrey I., Miguel Zaldivar and Richard Tewksbury (2014) "Breaking Out of Prison and into Print? Rationales and Strategies to Assist Educated Convicts Conduct Scholarly Research and Writing Behind Bars", *Critical Criminology*, Online First, 11 pages.

Schept, Judah (2014) "(Un)seeing Like a Prison: Counter-visual Ethnography of the Carceral State", *Theoretical Criminology*, 18(2): 198-223.

Simon, Jonathan (2014) "Ferguson and Human Dignity", *Social Justice Blog* – August 25. Retrieved from: <http://www.socialjusticejournal.org/?p=2491>.

Walmsley, Roy (2013) *World Prison Population List* (10th Edition), London: International Centre for Prison Studies. Retrieved from <http://www.prison studies.org/sites/prisonstudies.org/files/resources/downloads/wppl_10.pdf>.

From the Depths I Will Rise:
On Being Buried Alive and Survival
Anonymous

Several months ago I experienced something that I hope few will ever experience: I left a Supermax Prison in Colorado after spending 56 months in long-term solitary confinement. I had been buried alive, locked away from others. At first I was placed in 'the hole' because prison officials had deemed me too dangerous to be around others. Later, paperwork snafus and the release process kept me in my small cell until the day of my release. After so long in a sensory vacuum, I would find as much punishment from the first days of my release as I did from solitary. After all those years, the sights and sounds I had missed, the lack of people and touch, and even a simple conversation created a feeling of sensory overload.

The world of solitary confinement is an environment with detrimental effects that few people can comprehend. It was an experience that in a small way was like Phillip Zimbardo's infamous "Stanford Prison Experiment". However, this was no experiment. It was real life – no escape, no calling an end to anything because the subjects were going crazy, and no safety if you chose to complain that the authority figures were behaving immorally or unethically.

I sat by myself in a twelve-by-eight foot cell. I was a witness to mental abuse, physical abuse, suicide, literally watching grown men go insane, and on top of all that medical and psychological neglect. There was no escape. I did not have the option of saying "I've had enough" and expect to go home. I was stuck no matter how bad the situation got, no matter how the guards treated me, and no matter if I started to lose my mind. I was stuck with myself and my thoughts – that was it.

The mind does incredible and fascinating things to survive in such environments. I learned to withstand an emotional state and a level of loneliness I could have never even comprehended or understood prior to that experience. I learned very quickly how to be by myself and adapt to that state. I quite literally learned to depend on myself and myself only. I would go several days straight without something as simple as a shower if the facility was on lockdown. Learning to adapt to any and all environments and circumstances is one of the most intriguing and fascinating things I learned my mind and body could do. If you are treated like an animal long enough then you begin to think and act like one – that is what happened to me. I was fed my meals through a small slot in the door, handcuffed and shackled

4

before the door was opened to walk to the shower, locked in a cage for several days at a time with no fresh air, never any sunlight and very limited social interaction. Learn to live and depend on yourself or succumb to inner insanity. Being locked behind a steel door with only a small window to the outside world the feeling of hopelessness grows greater. Each and every day I felt less human, because everything that made me human – contact and conversations, walking in sunlight, and even the drive to find personal satisfaction and success – was taken away from me. The absence of other people meant an absence of self.

For me, I believe it is the fundamental purpose of our whole social existence to feel and be felt, to understand and be understood on a personal level, but such happenings do not occur in isolation. For me, the keys to survival were to stay busy with whatever I could find: reading, puzzles and writing letters. Daily exercise acted as a stress reliever and helped to enhance sleep at night. These activities also helped to convince me that I was still a human being with real feelings, emotions and thoughts. These activities gave me purpose to exist and gave me a reason to survive.

I did the same thing at the same time every day for five years. Every day I would wake-up before breakfast and do a small, but intense workout. After breakfast was served I would begin the process of preserving and strengthening my mind. This would normally include reading psychology, philosophy and economics. Around the time I finished my studies lunch would be served. After lunch, I would write a letter or two until lunch was digested. As soon as I was ready I would fill about two hours of my afternoon exercising in my cell. When the workout regimen was fulfilled I would take a "bird bath" in the sink in my cell. After washing up I would write a few more letters. I quickly found that communication to and from the outside world to those I love was my purest form of mental survival. By this time dinner was coming around and I would eat, and then spend the duration of the evening reading my books. Going to sleep early was a small way to guarantee myself some sleep. During the long nights in the box – between the doors constantly opening, guards' speaking over the loudspeakers, and the horrible sounds of people losing their minds and screaming in psychological agony – sleep was a precious commodity.

In spite of all these personal struggles I somehow left that tomb way better than I came in. I was handcuffed, shackled and double-escorted every time I left the cell. I was exposed to 24 hours of light and even flashlights in my eyes all night long. I ate and slept alone every day. I survived solitary, despite the harsh realities involved, but I was unfortunately one of the very few. What saved me was my desire to beat the system and show that I would not be broken. My mind became my refuge from the constant void of humanity, and the longer I was without sensory or mental stimulation the easier it was for me to dive into my own thoughts.

My exposure to long-term isolation was an experience of both sensory deprivation and, upon release, sensory overload. The human senses include sight, hearing, taste, smell, and touch, and when these senses are not used or are limited they become stagnant, almost non-reactive to stimuli. Sensory deprivation is a big part of what the authorities think will help to control violent and uncontrollable prisoners. When we are deprived of the sensory stimuli we so desperately need, it actually does the complete opposite of what is said to be intended: it does not tame us, it manufactures madness.

Seeing nothing but the four walls of a cell 24 hours a day not only makes you feel trapped, but it also severely limits the transfer of information to the brain and ultimately can prove to be detrimental to your eyesight. The eerie silence of isolation and the overall lack of auditory stimuli can also hamper and contribute to the loss of hearing. This is the same with taste and smell. As I learned in psychology class, if certain neural pathways and circuits are not used, the brain can lose them. I feel this proves that sensory deprivation can cause several impairments in our brain and senses in general.

My sense of touch was starved of for five long years. Losing the ability to touch and be touched, feel and be felt was the most detrimental part of the experience for me, along with others in my situation. At first you begin to convince yourself that you will do anything for human contact. Anything to feel alive, to feel something, including getting cell extracted just to have that contact. But after a while, when starved of physical contact for so long, you begin to fear it and want nothing to do with it, inducing further isolation not brought on by yourself, but by your environment.

Even the guards did not see us as human. Every guard on pretty much every shift was primed to deal with prisoners using premeditated and calculated humiliation. They called us names, destroyed our cells and private property, and would attempt at every corner to abuse their power and discourage us from communication, medical help, therapy, and visits with lawyers, family, and friends. If we fought back we could lose our already restricted privileges. As psychiatrist Stuart Grassian says, "[i]t's kind of like kicking and beating a dog and keeping it in a cage until it gets as crazy and vicious and wild as it can possibly get and then one day you take it out into the middle of the streets of New York or San Francisco and open the cage and you run away. That's no favor to the community or to the person" (Kamel and Kerness, 2003, p. 8). Their treatment of us often made us worse instead of better.

It is well documented and established that isolation and sensory deprivation can cause and enhance or even aggravate a variety of psychiatric symptoms. As documented in a briefing paper by the Humans Rights Watch "prisoners subjected to prolonged isolation may experience depression, despair, anxiety, rage, claustrophobia, hallucinations, problems with impulse control and an impaired ability to think, concentrate or remember" (ibid, p.3). I used to try and read a lot, but could never seem to be able to focus for longer than 30 minutes at a time. Even after long reading sessions I would have great difficulty remembering anything I had just read, which seems consistent with Kamel and Kerness' work.

Stuart Grassian, a lead psychiatrist at the Harvard Medical School and expert in the realm of the psychological impact of Supermax prisons, reports "the courts have recognized that long term solitary confinement itself can cause a very specific kind of psychiatric syndrome, which in its worst stages can lead to an agitated, hallucinatory, confusional state often involving random violence and self-mutilation, suicidal behavior and other agitated and fearful and confusional kinds of symptoms" (ibid). This mental condition is attributed to the sensory deprivation and sensory overload caused by solitary confinement, and this mental snake pit is where I fought to survive for over five long years.

When the effects of sensory deprivation set in after a year or so of extreme isolation, any and all stimuli became sensory overload. Simple things such as a change in cell locations or even a trip to the doctor were completely overwhelming and hard to deal with. It made me want to hide or close my eyes. The sudden assault of enraging sensory stimuli – the sound of loud doors opening and closing all day and night, flashlights in your eyes all night, 24-hour light in your cell, keys jingling on the guard's belt – all became much too loud and much too annoying. Intercoms and loudspeakers in the cells and pods would emit very loud noises and voices all day and night. The sounds become very overwhelming and they never went away. The visual and auditory senses would, at times, become overloaded to the point where I wanted the noise to stop. Yet I remained starved of taste, smell, and touch. It was a feeling of having nothing and having too much all at the same time. I can see how some prisoners went mad as a result. If I had not fought inside my mind, I might have lost myself altogether.

For me social interaction became non-existent after three years in isolation. It became too much to handle. Even simple conversation with a guard or a prisoner down the tier was so mentally challenging and overwhelming I chose not to engage in it. Being by myself and keeping to myself was all I felt comfortable doing. It was as if my environment did not isolate me enough from others and after even more time I began to isolate myself from myself. It is no mystery that humans are social animals. Our whole social identity is formed based on our social interaction with others.

Psychology professor Harry Harlow tested the social impact of isolation with baby rhesus monkeys. The researchers found that upon being released into a group of ordinary monkeys the test monkeys "usually go into a state of emotional shock, characterized by ... autistic self-clutching and rocking, 12 months of isolation almost completely obliterated the animals socially" (Gawande, 2012, p. 2). Moreover, "EEG studies going back to the 1960's have shown diffuse slowing of brain waves in prisoners after a week or more of solitary confinement reports the New Yorker"(ibid, p. 3). Another professor, Craig Haney, from the University of California Santa Cruz, notes "that after months or years of complete isolation many prisoners begin to lose the ability to initiate behavior of any kind – to organize their own lives around activity and purpose. Chronic apathy, lethargy, depression, and despair often result... in extreme cases prisoners may literally stop behaving, becoming essentially catatonic" (ibid, p. 5). Haney also found " that 90% of these prisoners had difficulties with irrational anger compared with just 3% of the general population", which he linked "to the extreme restriction, the totality of control and the extended absence of any opportunity for happiness of joy" (ibid).

When you completely lose the capacity to make any choice for yourself and can make no choices for yourself or your survival, your mind begins to do something that you have little control over – it begins to crack. Pacing is what prisoners called it. Walking back and forth from the bed to the door, the door to the bed for a couple of hours every day; it was a terrible feeling, yet it was a means of escape. It took my mind outside those four walls for a little while. Day after day it felt like the wall that kept me in were the same walls that seem to be closing in on my mind, trying to suffocate my very being. There was no social interaction – no pleasure of relationships, no talking, no touching, and no laughing. The majority of happiness one achieves or experiences during his or her life-time is usually attributed to the friendship or the relationships that they have. When I became stripped of that I lost all sense of joy. My feelings evolved into a state of sadness that later morphed into full-on loneliness and depression. I began to shut down mentally and physically.

After several years in solitary confinement I had adjusted to the lack of everything. My socially nonexistent world became routine, so my return to the world outside the prison became a lot more challenging. I had lost the majority of my social skills. Upon my release from solitary after 56 months I experienced feelings and sensations I had never felt before: extreme paranoia, anxiety, nervousness, vulnerability and loss of confidence in all social situations. I could not hold face-to-face conversations, could not be in small rooms, could not be around more than four to five people at a time, and even felt very nervous being in public places. These are feelings no human should ever feel.

I have always been a very social person, loved talking to people, and interacting with those around me, but these days, eight months after my release, I still lack complete confidence in many social situations. I still like to sit with my back in the corner of a room, but I am getting better. My hands still sweat when I meet someone I do not know and I am still a bit hesitant to engage in face-to-face conversations with total strangers. However, with a strong desire to get all my social skills back I try to do all these things as often as possible. I am adjusting to normal life outside the tomb of isolation, but I am scared my life will never be in full fashion, never again back to the "normal" so many people take for granted.

My solitary confinement experience was the hardest thing I had ever endured up to that point in my life. Adjusting to life in society, being around people and accepting new responsibilities is even harder. Yet because of my struggle I have found strength I never knew I had and am now an even firmer believer in free will. Because of my five years in the box my life is now better than it has ever been, mainly because I value and appreciate everything, every little experience. From a simple sunrise to the ability to make choices for myself, normal sensory input and social interaction on a daily basis make life so grand. Living with nothing teaches you to appreciate everything, and I mean everything. Being deprived and flooded with sensory stimulation at the same time is very detrimental to one's psychological state. Being exposed to solitary conditions is both physically and emotional damaging, and the short- and long-term impact of the deterioration of social skills is the harshest of all. Anxiety, nervousness, headaches, chronic tiredness, loss of sleep, trouble sleeping, impending nervous breakdown, perspiring hands, loss of appetite, dizziness, nightmares, and shaky hands are some of the symptoms of psychological and emotional trauma I experienced.

Articles regarding solitary confinement and the effects of prison show that I am not the only one who went through hell (see Piché and Major, forthcoming), both during my time in isolation and after my release. The psychopathological effects of prolonged isolation are ruminations, irrational anger, over sensitivity to stimuli, confused thought processes, social withdrawal, chronic depression, emotional flatness, crazy mood swings, overall deterioration, talking to yourself, violent fantasies, perceptual distortions, hallucinations and suicidal thoughts. For five years I was buried alive. My body was in prison, my mind in hell, and although, upon my release my body was allowed to leave my cement tomb, my mind continued and still continues to be trapped inside a prison created by isolation and sensory deprivation. "Living behind these and inside those four small walls is a nightmare that never goes away! Many of us behind these walls are going crazy in record numbers and are becoming more damaged and more violent than we have ever been in our whole lives. What good is that to society?" (California SHU Prisoner in Magnani, 2008, p. 9). In spite all of it all, I will rise!

REFERENCES

Gawande, Atul (2012) "Hellhole", *The New Yorker – Annals of Human Rights*.

Kamel, Rachel and Bonnie Kerness (2003) *The Prison Inside the Prison: Control Units, Supermax Prisons, and Devices of Torture*, Philadelphia: American Friends Service Committee.

Magnani, Laura (2008) Buried Alive: Long-Term Isolation in California's Youth and Adult Prisons, Oakland: American Friends Service Committee.

Piché, Justin and Karine Major (forthcoming) "Prisoner Writing in/on Solitary Confinement: Contributions from the Journal of Prisoners on Prisons, 1988-2013", *Canadian Journal of Human Rights*.

Weiten, Wayne (2008) *Psychology: Scenes and Variations* (8th edition), Belmont: Wadsworth.

ABOUT THE AUTHOR

Anonymous is now a former Colorado state prisoner who runs his own successful catering business in the United States. Having survived solitary confinement, he is working through the transition of living a life where his senses are fully engaged, including as a first-time father of a soon to be born baby girl.

Institutionalized Indifference:
Rape with a View
Michael Johnson Jr.

INTRODUCTION

In this essay, I discuss my experience with institutional indifference during a brief stay at a medium security local jail in Southeastern Louisiana and the conditions, circumstances and participants involved in my sexual assault. In this discussion, I intend to offer an "insider's account" as a type of autoethnographic method of inquiry whose purpose is to expose readers to the complex dynamics of life within a correctional system for a young, middle class, college educated, gay[1] man of colour. This "insider's account" attempts to describe the conditions and circumstances of my incarceration, which contributed to my sexual assault and the ensuing analysis of that event.

I begin with a discussion of my methodology, specifically my decision to employ the autoethnographic method and the application of "convict criminology" in the elaboration of my personal narrative. Then, I present that narrative – which describes my experiences while incarcerated that lead up to and included my assault – followed by some analysis about prison culture, both general and specific to the institution where I was held, in tandem with an exploration of prison sex and sexual culture, and the discourses of safety that proliferate outside its walls. Finally, I conclude with a discussion about the politics of prison rape and sexual assault that include a summary of, and my personal reactions subsequent to, my escape and release from both the institution and my attacker. The objective in writing this essay is to better inform readers about the socioeconomic, racist and homophobic obstacles that faces those familiar and unfamiliar with our Nation's criminal justice system and the very real, very frightening problems of sexual assault that gay men must encounter and negotiate – every day, of every week, of every year within that system.

WRITING, REMEMBERING AND RELIVING:
METHODOLOGY

I adopt convict criminology's theoretical objectives to "honestly declare who we are, to articulate what we experienced and observed and to do ethnography that tells the truth" (Ross and Richards, 2009). And because "convicts are rarely asked to comment on prison policy or procedure" (Ross 2003, 243) I hope that my story will also render myself visible as a survivor. Methodologically, I have adopted an autoethnographic approach for the purposes of this research because it offers both a personal narrative and an analytical assessment of the events surrounding my incarceration and assault (Anderson, 2006). My objective here is to "document...and bear witness to harmful social practices, occasions of relational violence" (Adams and Jones, 2011, p. 111) that I have overcome, and to provide an "insider's" account.

My decision to embrace the autoethnographic method is based on the firm belief that autoethnography can offer an invaluable, evocative, personal narrative that – when combined with scholarly inquiry and rigorous intellectual analysis – can produce insightful qualitative results that might otherwise go un(der)investigated, unobserved and un(der)theorized (Ellis, Adams and Bochner, 2011). By explicitly incorporating a personal narrative, especially as I do here with an "insider's" perspective, autoethnography creates a theoretical platform from which analyses of that narrative can be undertaken (Gatson, 2003). Moreover, Norman Denzin (1997, p. 228) writes that evocative autoethnographers "bypass the representational problem by invoking an epistemology of emotion, moving the reader to feel the feelings of the other". Denzin's observations are particularly important here, since the retelling of my story – despite the pain and shame of its remembrance – functions as a way to make sense of my experience, as much as it is a means to raise the visibility of same-sex rape – a subject woefully in need of much more public attention and scholarly investigation (Kunzel, 2008).

To tell my story, I draw on a wide variety of source materials, including correspondence written during my incarceration to, and the replies from, various agencies and people, personal notes, recorded telephone conversations between my attorney and myself, district court records, and my own memories. One of the most substantial limitations to the use of memories is the fact that I suffer from an "inability to recall an important aspect of the trauma" (Turner, 1992). Despite the passage of years, I still want to forget the *specific details* of my assault, however successfully I can recount them for readers here. The images, smells, sounds and minutiae of the people, places and locations during my brief incarceration bring with them the ever attendant antagonisms of shame and humiliation that accompany such recollections. Although some might argue that there is a therapeutic benefit in the recounting of my assault, I have yet to find that to be true. There is a peace and solitude in the silence that comes with forgetting. However, I have temporarily accepted, for the purpose of this work, to forego the insulating comfort which comes from that solitude to make my story known.

RAPE, INVISIBILITY AND
INSTITUTIONAL COMPLICITY

Regina Kunzel (2008) explains that rape is such a well-known, commonsensical component of prison life that it inevitability shapes the expectations of those sentenced to prison. Sexual violence in prison is so well known that its inclusion in novels, plays and films constitute a frame of reference to which American society constantly refers when invoking ideas of incarceration (ibid, 155). However, the acceptance and circulation of these discourses in popular culture often omit the voices, experiences and existence of the men who are sexually abused (some of whom are gay men). Indeed, within the perverse sexual culture of same sex prisons, prisoners do not label a behaviour as rape "unless those acts meet particular conditions set by inmate culture's construction of rape" (Fleisher and Krienert, 2009, p. 85). The common definition of rape is interpreted as "sexual relations with another person obtained through physical force, threats or intimidation...rape is forcible sexual assault" (Scacco, 1982, p. 231). Despite this commonsensical understanding, the definitions of terms like "'rape', 'sexual assault', 'sodomy', 'sexual abuse', and 'coercive sex' have taken on expanded meanings, which can even differ depending upon the perspective (medical, legal, etc.) being employed" (Kunselman, *et al.*, 2002, p. 28). Thus, there is a wide discrepancy between what constitutes rape, *who can be* raped, and where and when it can be expected to occur.

Moreover, perpetrators of prison rape "almost never face criminal charges" (Mariner, 2003, p. 232) such was the case with my attacker. I continue to question how this reality can be reconciled with the presumption articulated by the US Supreme Court that "being violently assaulted in prison is simply not part of the penalty that criminal offenders pay for their offenses against society" and that "prison rape not only threatens the lives of those who fall prey to their aggressors, but is potentially devastating to the human spirit. Shame, depression, and a shattering loss of self-esteem accompany the perpetual terror the victim thereafter must endure" (Farmer V. Brennan, 1994). Rape, by prisoners' accounts, is no aberrational occurrence. Instead, it is a deeply-rooted, systemic problem. It is also a problem that prison authorities do little to address. Rape plagues American prisons "because of a lack of attention or concern by prison authorities or politicians. In too many institutions, prevention measures are meager and effective punishment of abuses is rare" (Mariner, 2003, p. 232).

Although my facility was an exception, most states do not have facilities capable of accommodating safe separate housing for lesbian, gay and transgender prisoners, primarily due to cost, lack of space and the small population size. As such, they are at a "heightened risk of abuse...leaving prisoners open to harassment and violence" and because prison staff are afforded 'unfettered discretion', this only "contributes to their systematic victimization" (Tarzwell, 2006, p. 17). And yet according to Mariner (2003, p. 232), "the federal courts have played an insignificant role in curtailing prisoner-on-prisoner rape" despite a responsibility for prisoner safety recognized by the US Supreme Court. The court *unanimously* stated that "prison officials have a duty under the Eighth Amendment[2] to refrain from indifference as to prisoners' safety with regard to violence and assault by other prisoners...having stripped [them] of virtually every means of self-protection and foreclosed their access to outside aid, the government and its officials are not free to let the state of nature [sic] take its course" and that "gratuitously allowing the beating or rape of one prisoner by another serves no legitimate penological objective" (Farmer V. Brennan, 1994). Despite that obligation only twenty-five states even keep statistical records of rape incidents and of those just six stated that their correctional officers receive specialized training in recognizing or preventing prisoner sexual assault (Mariner, 2003, p. 234).

AN OBJECT LESSON IN HUMILIATION

November 1996

My story began on what seemed to be a very long car ride, in the back seat of a police cruiser on the way to jail late in the afternoon. The facility I was travelling to was not really a "prison", but a medium security county facility in Southeast Louisiana that housed about 1500 prisoners (1410 males and 184 females) and employed approximately 350 Sherriff's deputies. Earlier that day, I had been caught shoplifting three textbooks in the bookstore, while attending

Louisiana State University as an undergraduate. I was a 6 foot 1, 180 pound, thin, 21 year old Latino undergraduate college student, in a state where college graduates constitute only 21 percent of society, and the vast majority of whom are white (Complete College America, 2011). While I was phenotypically classified as white within the complex hierarchy of the state's racially intricate history, my skin is brown. My facial features and jet Black hair, and acute verbal locution characterized me as a Caucasian and consequently I benefitted from the privilege that such an assignment brings with it in the racial hierarchy of southern Louisiana culture. Despite these complex "advantages" I was a young man with a pencil thin mustache, gold rimmed glasses and a soft spoken, but articulate insouciance towards authority. Thus, I knew that my fate was sealed the moment the cruiser left the station on its journey towards the local jail. And most importantly, I was openly gay.

I arrived at a low, cement brick walled facility surrounded by what I thought was "barbed wire", but in actuality was "concertina wire" and a long chain link fence. The gates opened slowly and we pulled into a loading bay. Trying to compose myself I climbed out of the car, with the police officer's help, his strong hand on my arm, he guided me toward the sally port of the facility's booking section. I was next interviewed by another white male deputy, who sat next to an ancient monochromatic green computer screen, who began to ask me a series of questions. I later learned that this was where I was classified, based on a variety of factors that included criminal history (none), race ("white" according to the arrest report and other booking documents), age (21), education (undergraduate), booking agency (LSU – I later learned that their appearance at the facility was an infrequent occurrence and was one that deputies noticed), charge (felony theft) and a number of other things. Finally during this debriefing of sorts, I was asked that magical question – "Are you homosexual or bisexual?" to which I replied "yes". The deputy, who had been asking these questions, had been looking down the entire time, writing my responses down on his checklist. At that precise moment, he finally looked up; he began to *really look* at me, and I just stood there, curiously wondering why he suddenly was taking an interest in me and if my answer to this last question was the reason.

He turned away for a split second and then looked back at me and said "ok" just sit down here (next to him). I sat back down on the wooden bench separated from the main central booking area adjacent to this office. After a few moments of typing, during which I thought his typing skills were in serious need of attention, I was taken into the main central booking area (surrounded by the large, multi-person cells). The classification deputy spoke to the deputy on duty and handed over my paperwork. This duty deputy (another white man, albeit with a very pink, completely skin shaved head) rose from his chair in the control platform and took me towards the multi-person cell, whereupon the booking deputy (who had begun to walk away) turned and loudly yelled "he's L2, put him in cell 4!" The booking deputy immediately changed course, his left hand firmly grasping my right arm and proceeded to a flank of single man cells directly in front of the control platform, one of which, painted pink, was filled with women. And the cell next to it, also painted pink, was where I was unceremoniously, but gently pushed into.

After retreating to the back of the cell on its wooden bench, out of the sight of almost all of the Central Booking prisoner's view, I tried to compose myself and decipher how I was going to extricate myself from this situation. Moments later, a young guy (around my age) walked up to the front of my cell and asked me to come forward to speak with him. I remember thinking that he was cute in his jeans and LSU pullover and ball cap, dressed as he was in something other than the tan and green uniforms of the sheriff deputies that I had encountered so far. He interviewed me for bail and went about explaining the process of being assigned bail. He looked in my eyes and spoke softly but clearly and it was the first time that night that anyone had treated me even remotely humanely. Until that moment, I had been shuffled, pushed, and pulled into, out of and around the room and patrol car. He informed me that I would be taken into an adjacent room with a closed circuit television and microphone where I would be presented to a judge who would have a report (prepared by him) that would determine the price of my bail. He explained that it would probably be around $10,000 of which I would have to raise 10% or $1,000.00 if I used a bail bondsman, and I was given the opportunity to make a telephone call. I asked few questions, but remember thinking that he was the first person to actually use my name the entire time. And here is where my story truly begins. I never left the facility until after I went to court four weeks later. And the simple reason is that pay phones cannot call cell phones and ironically, everyone I knew at the time only had a cell phone. *All my family, friends, and even my dorm roommates* only had cell phones. And I did not remember a single phone number. Had I remembered *just one phone number* I would have been able to leave that evening or at the latest the next day. It was only until I finally got to court and spoke with an attorney who could call my family and friends, was I finally able to leave, but by that point my life had already changed – as you will soon learn.

Since I was unable to make bail, I was escorted to a changing room where my clothing and property was inventoried. This included my cell phone and as much as I begged and pleaded I was not allowed to touch it much less turn it on and search for any phone numbers – which is still a source of anger almost profound as that produced from my physical attack. I was given a receipt, a prison uniform, a blanket, towels and miscellaneous hygiene products, and a prisoner handbook outlining the facilities rules and regulations. I was escorted back to my pink cell and being a voracious reader, I quickly consumed the handbook and realized that there was nothing to do amidst the noise and clamor of central booking. I eventually struck up a conversation through the bars with the women adjacent to me and they were uniformly very polite and courteous, which I found to be particularly heartwarming in my circumstances at the time. They were all very nice, but were obviously all from socioeconomically depressed backgrounds, despite being evenly divided between Black and white racial groups. The time passed slowly until just after "dinner" when I was eventually escorted to my final "home away from home" on L2.

L2 was the designation for the homosexual wing. It was a small, squat cement brick building just like the rest of the facility. Yet, it was physically separate, as one had to walk through a caged walkway outside the main facility into the open air and walk down a paved cement sidewalk to its front door, where one had to be buzzed in. It had sliding inner and outer brown metal doors. The inner door opened to a large rectangular room with one wall dedicated to a single row of steel bunk beds with plastic mattresses. In the middle was a metal table and at one end a shower and a steel emergency exit. On the wall directly opposite to the row of bunk beds was a colour television affixed to a metal stand on the wall and close to the shower, sat a long metal urinal and a single metal toilet. There were ten bunk beds and at the time of my incarceration there were about twelve people there – all but three of whom were Black men – the others were Caucasian men around the age of 30-40. I sat down and was immediately approached by what appeared to be a Black transsexual who courteously introduced herself as Ms. Goldie.

Ms. Goldie was an older Black male around the age of 40-45 from my estimation. Ms. Goldie and I spoke briefly and I was introduced to the prisoners as Michael and given a choice of locations to sleep. This decision proved to be very important within the hierarchical dynamics of the L2 community. I chose a bottom bunk with a corner wall (apparently coveted real estate) whose feet faced the door. My bunkmate "upstairs" was a very kind and gentle Black man, around the age of 45 or 48 who, like all the rest of the Black men on L2 were imprisoned primarily on prostitution charges. L2 proved to be the one *(and only)* place within the facility where I was truly safe. And it was here that my education about prison culture commenced.

Not a single prisoner on L2 was imprisoned for a violent crime and during my stay there never was one. Indeed, it was the one reason why we were treated fairly decently as we posed no physical threat to the deputies who worked in our building or at the facility at large. Apart from medical call, visitation, court appearances or the cafeteria we never left L2. Mail was delivered daily and commissary once a week. To my knowledge, I was the only person to ever leave L2 for any other reason (due to my Spanish linguistic abilities, I was often called upon to be a translator). Normally, this would have produced envy and vindictiveness, but it turned out to be a cause célèbre as I was able to carry paper notes to other prisoners on my way through the facility to central booking where the medical ward was located. Thus, what normally might have been perceived as a distinct disadvantage turned out to be something valued by my fellow prisoners. Communication with other prisoners was impossible given our little building being physically separated from the rest of the facility. As Mark Fleisher (2009, p. 66) makes clear:

> In prison, the labels 'gay' and 'straight' are not necessarily mutually exclusive categories... two basic sexual tracks can be forged. The first involves openly homosexual behavior; actors in these categories define themselves as homosexuals and are considered homosexuals by the prison culture. The second track contains men who define themselves as straight, but may or may not participate in sexual acts with other men. Regardless of their behavior, they are seen as heterosexual by member of the prison culture. A separate hierarchy exists for each sexual track.

December 1996

I was finally being transported to court for my arraignment. I was looking forward to it because I knew that I would be assigned at least a public defender and thus, I would be given an opportunity to speak with someone (anyone) about getting in touch with my friends and family to arrange for my bail. I actually was elated when, before breakfast, the deputy working on L2 announced my name on the court "call out" list (which meant we were to leave the facility immediately after breakfast). Shocked at hearing my name, I quickly began asking people questions about what to expect, where I would go, how long would it take and so on. while trying to get dressed at the same time and make myself look presentable to the judge and the court in general. I was nervous as hell and anxious to get on the road. After breakfast, they called me out and sat me on a hallway bench while other prisoners heading to court went into a large multi-person cell off the main hallway. While they were being handcuffed and shackled in a humiliating display of barbarity, I was handcuffed only because shackling would require that I be paired to another prisoner (though I understand that this did happen on those rare occasions when more than one L2 prisoner was attending court on the same day, and thus could be paired together).

Soon I was, as usual, escorted to the head of the line at one end of the hall with a deputy, to the hooting, hollering and whistles of the men aligned against the wall. We walked through the facility and out into the daylight. I recall the vividness of the colours outside that early morning and remembered that I still had a life waiting for me if I could ever legally escape the current circumstances of my confinement. We travelled by bus to the courthouse, entering via an underground parking garage into holding tank level. I was housed in a much smaller adjacent cell (inside a larger office) next to the female prisoners who, despite my nervousness, actually made the interminable wait tolerable. Sometimes men would flash themselves at us between moments when deputies were not in the office. While this made me very uncomfortable, I did what I usually did on these innumerable occasions and tried to ignore them. If there is one thing that you'll learn about the criminal justice system in Louisiana is it *moves slowly*. We arrived around 7:00 am and I did not appear in court until 3:00 pm.

I, along with two deputies and approximately six other men were escorted to a commercial, loading dock type elevator, packed in together like sardines.

One deputy was with me at all times, while the other unshackled and escorted the various prisoners to their respective courtroom floors. Finally, I was the last and only one remaining in the elevator and I too arrived at my destination. I stepped off the elevator and was escorted down a hallway that divided the courtrooms from the Judge's chambers and various offices. At the end of the hallway was a jury deliberation room where I was told to sit down and was handcuffed to the chair. I remember looking outside the window from the 11th floor judge's courtroom – the view was amazing. I also recall how luxurious the furnishing were for its padded, fabric seats seems to be from another world and, as I rocked back and forth, I began to uncomfortably think about what I had been missing. One does not miss the simple things until they are taken away. At the end of this hallway was a type of elevated platform with a U-shaped desk and multiple Black and white monitors.

There stood an older Black man – a captain by rank who yelled frequently to other deputies and wore a perpetual scowl. Not more than five minutes passed before he accosted me and angrily asked "what the fuck are you doing out here?!" To which I responded, I was waiting to be called into court for my appearance. He immediately seized a junior deputy, a young man, no more than 45 years old and said "put him in the tank". Fear ran down my spine and I instantaneously felt nauseous and it was the only time in my life I felt like I might urinate on myself. I said "No! I can't go in there!" and the Captain simultaneously yelled over me to "shut up" and said "put his ass in there [pointing to the tank] right now".

The tank was a large holding cell with a solid steel door and a tiny Plexiglas window with a steel shutter that covered the window. The junior deputy started towards me with his face down and began to uncuff me from the seat. I began to cry and said over and over again, "please, you can't put me in there! I'm gay! I'm on L2; you can't put me in there". My pleas falling on deaf ears, the Captain simply yelled to "hurry up" to the deputy as he literally dragged me as I struggled against him towards the door. He quickly pushed me inside the room, his face never meeting mine. I felt that *he knew* what he was doing was wrong. As the door started to close I turned around and saw three young Black men seated on a metal bench that ran the perimeter of the tank on three walls. There was one toilet, a light in the ceiling and nothing else. It was entirely too close for comfort. I had 'lived' in the relative safety of L2 during the weeks of my incarceration. Now, at that moment, I truly realized the real danger that I was in.

One young man with braids, named "redbone" was in for Murder, the second young man named "Black" was incarcerated for Burglary and Aggravated Assault, the third whose name I can't recall, was incarcerated for a series of high value thefts. In what seemed to be an eternity, but probably lasted only 15 minutes, I endured subtle but unmistakable harassment that gained in intensity as time passed, from questions to threats to sexual suggestions. Although the conversation started with friendly chitchat about each person's legal case that brought them to court appearance that day, it quickly escalated despite my feeble attempts to change topics. "Redbone" quickly became aggressive, although "Black" and the other remained relatively subdued. Within minutes, I was so uncomfortable I grabbed "Black's" bible sitting next to him and began to pray out loud, thinking that this might dissuade "Redbone" and his attraction. It did not. He then stood up and approached me from the opposite side of small cell, snatched the bible out of my hands and threw it back to "Black", pulled his pants down and demanded that I perform oral sex.

I was eventually pushed in the corner where the toilet was located and he began to assault me. It was not a rape that one sees in a movie, but a slow, methodical type of process accompanied by whispered threats. Because of the confined space and the frequency of prisoners being moved in and out of the cell, oral sex was the only option. I briefly thought of biting him, but was warned that I would quickly lose all my teeth. After a few minutes, though an eternity of agony, I realized through my tears that I was within reach of the metal door. I banged on that door as fast and as quick as I could, since I knew my arms would immediately be pinned after my attempt so I would not be able to reach it again. Fortunately, the slot on the window opened which forced him to back away, knowing that people could see inside motivated him to move back to the far corner of the cell. Suddenly, but temporarily free, I yelled for help. This immediately brought the joyous sounds of keys being rattled in the lock and "Redbone" quickly ran back across the tank. The violation itself lasted no more than 2-3 minutes and I moved to the doorway and saw the junior deputy. I whispered to him what just happened and he immediately moved me out of the tank and back into the jury deliberation room. Thankfully, the Captain was nowhere to be seen.[4]

After he handcuffed me to the chair, he knelt down, looked me in the eye, put his hand on my shoulder and asked, "Are you okay?" I hoarsely mumbled through utterly distraught tears and sobbing that "I was okay now". He then left the room and came back with two Dixie cups of water and asked if I wanted some more to which I replied, "No, but please don't put me back there again". I recall him standing up, and looking down at me, saying "No, I won't put you back in there, no matter what". Much to my regret, I cannot remember his name although I believe it was Italian, but I will *never* forget his face. He then apologized (which for a brief moment, shocked me to the core) and said that he had to leave and go back to his station, whereupon he left me alone. He said that the courtroom deputy would eventually retrieve me when the time came, and until then I would be left alone to wait for my court appearance. Composing myself, I took stock of my surroundings. I was sitting in a very comfortable, padded swivel chair, with wooden arms positioned at a long rectangular table surrounded by a number of chairs exactly like my own. As I sat there, feeling used and abused, my throat sore, hands trembling and sweat dripping down the insides of my undershirt, it almost felt surreal watching birds fly around outside as the world went by and the traffic on the I-10 Mississippi River Bridge moved like little toy cars back and forth across its span. The tears dried on my face and I felt a profound numbness inside. At that moment, I really did not care what was going to happen to me in the courtroom. I just needed to get out.

I only saw my rescuer once more (though he did not see me), as I was later escorted out of the courtroom and into the hallway, chained and handcuffed to another person as we walked, clink, clink, clink towards the elevator. A day after my court appearance, I was released. Days later, I mustered the courage to report the incident to the Sherriff Department's Internal Affairs office. I met with overweight white man, dressed in plain clothes at the Sherriff's downtown headquarters in a cramped hot office. The room reeked of smoke and stale coffee, and every possible surface was covered with piles and piles of manila folders and papers. I thought I was on a movie set, but it was real life. The man sat there as I told my story, taking a few handwritten notes as both he and I sat in the stifling heat. Finally, after an agonizing, emotionally draining hour, he looked up from his notepad and said "Ok, I'll see what I can do". He did not ask any questions. No, he did not need any additional information, and yes he had my contact information.

I left thinking reporting it was a complete and total waste of time. As I walked outside, into the fresh air, I felt victimized all over again. A fresh sense of intense shame, anxiety, anger and despair pulsed through my veins with each heartbeat. I never heard from anyone in Internal Affairs again.

I count myself lucky, as my assault was relatively brief, I did not contract HIV or any STDs and I escaped mostly unscathed. But others are not so lucky. Had the location been different and the circumstances slightly more favourable for the perpetrator, what happened could have been much worse.

PRISON SEXUAL CULTURE AND HETERONORMATIVE HIERARCHIES

King (1992, p. 68) explains it is difficult to "separate sexual arousal from a desire for domination and aggression, but there is little doubt that sexual gratification plays a greater role in coercive sexual activity in prisons" than in free society. Of particular importance to my own experience, Scacco (1982, p. 5) has long recognized that the "pursuit of power via sexual violence and the enslavement of weaker prisoners is not peculiar to the Louisiana penal system. It is an integral feature of imprisonment throughout the United States".

The state of contemporary research into prison rape is abysmal. English and Heil (2005, p. 1) note that what little scholarly evidence *is* available "has failed to be translated to effective intervention strategies for treating inmate victims and ensuring improved correctional practices and management". Regardless of the paucity of scholarly knowledge about the prevalence, frequency or other data regarding prison sexual assault, Louisiana's correctional system needs to recognize that prison rape is real, that it happens, and that the obfuscation and denial that resulted in my case is not a legitimate solution to the problem. While incarcerated I had little recourse, either before or immediately after my assault, to adequately challenge the correctional system's responsiveness (or lack thereof) to the conditions that gay men must endure. And some of those conditions were a product not simply of the coercive nature that accompanies confinement of gay men within a heteronormative system, but also accompanies the well-known, but invisible preference of the largely heteronormative administration of the correctional system that barely tolerates our existence as an undesirable, but unavoidable demographic amongst the prison population.

As an out gay man, my nonconformity with the rigidly imposed sexual scripts and expected prison performances of heteronormativity were too ambiguous and too peripheral to fit within the convenient stereotypes of what "queens" were supposed to embody, thus (unknowingly) made me a target. I was regularly harassed by older Black prisoners when being escorted in the hallways with phrases like "know you place bitch, shave that shit off" (referring to my unwillingness to shave off my mustache) and "take that bass outta your voice". Somewhat contradictorily, very young Black men, who overwhelmingly outnumbered their older counterparts, would not make such comments preferring instead to try for even the briefest physical contact. In one case, a 22 year old boy constantly tried to kiss me – even in front of his older peers, which (amazingly) provoked little response from them.

His behaviour seemed to suggest that while there was undoubtedly a strict heteronormativity amongst the older demographic of Black men, younger Black male prisoners were afforded more apparent freedoms to violate these sexual scripts by virtue of their being "short timers" with little experience in the prison sex culture. Ironically, the heterosexual restrictions on prison sexual culture also extended to a perverse type of homonormative enforcement amongst and between other *gay men*. Some queens on L2 repeatedly told me to "sit down when you pee" in case "the men" (meaning other straight prisoners) saw me urinating, as standing up was what "men" (read heteronormatively) did and were they to see me standing up urinating, I might very well get hit without notice. These disciplining tactics reflect that of the prison hierarchy. More importantly, my unwillingness and abject rejection of those distorted norms and values made me a target, as my conduct and very appearance created an image of rebellion, thus publically threatening to destabilize the heteronormative prison sexual culture that renders gay men at the bottom of the hierarchy.

Although I suffered some mild bruising around the neck, as a consequence of attempting to resist, such "submission injuries" were far less pronounced than they could have been had I not been rescued when I was. The most pronounced effects of my assault were not physical but emotional. And as Richard Tewksbury (2000, p. 29) attests, "the most common emotional response of men to sexual assault victimization is a sense of stigma, shame and embarrassment...clearly shame is directly tied to frequent expressions of self-blame from victims and importantly serves to inhibit reporting or seeking of medical or mental health services". Despite Tewksbury's analysis that the feelings of shame stem from blame that we "victims" – a word I despise for its connotations of passive victimization – assign ourselves, the fact remains that shame is a powerful force. I have struggled for many months, trying to decide if I really wanted to pursue publication of this research and my narrative within it, specifically because of the damn near suffocating enormity of the shame that accompanies such public airing of a deeply stigmatizing event in my life. My reluctance stems not simply from the shame associated with the publicity that will accompany the publication of this research, but more importantly the potent fear of embarrassment that I worry will be paralyzing despite how valuable others might find this knowledge. Ultimately, I am hoping that the reward will come from knowing that silence shall have no power over me and that maybe other people will learn from this, my fragile display of courage.

YOU CAN'T BE RAPED IF YOU'RE A MAN

Knowles (1999, p. 273) accurately observes:

> One of the perverse mores in the world of prison is that victims of sexual violence are rarely regarded as 'victims'. A key element of the prisoners' belief system is that a 'man' cannot be forced to do anything that he does not want to do – a 'real man' cannot be exploited. Those unable to meet the stringent demands of that standard are regarded as not being 'men', but rather as being weak and unworthy of respect from those who *are* 'men'".

And without a doubt gay men like me at that age, and with my level of inexperience of prison culture, fall directly within this perverse catch 22.

To make things even worse, the "degree of satisfaction derived from the sex act is often in direct proportion to the degree of force and humiliation to which the partner is subjected" (Wooden & Parker, 1982) and this is especially the case in a world where the capacity to exercise violence is interpreted as a distinctly masculine (e.g. heterosexual) trait. At the facility level prison staff may "dismiss the victimized prisoner as merely engaging in 'gay' behavior (the implication being that gay men cannot be raped because they always consent to sex)" (Mariner, 2003, p. 237). Particularly discouraging is the fact that "[t]he courts have also made bizarre rulings defining an attack as not 'bona fide rape' if a condom is used. Specifically, the rulings suggest that if a victim can persuade an attacker to use a condom, it may be interpreted as a vague form of consent on the part of the victim" (Knowles, 1999, p. 270). Given these obstacles, it is surprising that more gay men in my dormitory were not sexually assaulted even in the relatively brief period of time while I lived on L2.

CORRECTIONAL OFFICERS AND PROFESSIONAL CULTURE

Many deputies were quite professional and vigilant in their duties, especially if we had personal relationships with them. But a few were not and they viewed their task with disdain, either because of personal animosity and homophobia or they believed the policy inherently flawed (granting special privilege). My experiences with correctional staff have been validated in much of the literature. In the sociocultural landscape of southeastern Louisiana, those who disliked gay men and the policies existing to protect them often found ways to circumvent their responsibilities – a common tactic would be to profess more important work priorities, thereby neglecting duties to protect our vulnerable population to sexual predation.

It is well established that many correctional officers "attitudes about rape influence their willingness to respond to rapes and many officers hold very stereotyped views on...homosexuality, together with their degree of religiosity, explain most of the variation in officer's willingness to respond to reported rapes" (Tewksbury and West, 2000, p. 373). In my experience, however, while Tewksbury's argument is true, race and age proved to be more influential predictors of correctional staff's willingness to respond to an actual rape.

The deputy who rescued me was a young man by comparison to the higher ranked Captain who thought that I was using my sexuality as a means to achieve some nefarious end, like sitting in a back hallway handcuffed to a chair. My rescuer was a younger, white deputy, while his superior was an older (almost elderly appearing) Black man with a particularly obvious dislike and revulsion towards my identifiably gay presence. I attribute the younger deputy's familiarity with gay men to his willingness to help me and, thus, this generational difference manifested itself in disastrous consequences in my case. Even in cases where correctional officers are present and aware that a sexual assault has taken place, "as long as there is no visible physical injury, prison guards will often stand by and suggest that the alleged rape was in fact consensual sex, simply because the prisoner was considered 'weak' and not strong enough to repel such victimization. In many cases prison officials just turn away and pretend that such violence is not really occurring (Crawford, 2001).

I was fortunate to some degree that my rescuer did not ignore my pleas and saved me from further brutalization. He was the only one who obviously understood my precarious position and sufficiently empathized with my plight to intercede on my behalf despite the potential professional consequences – and because of that I was very lucky. But at the same time, while he was sensitive and caring to me in the immediate aftermath, it was obvious that he was neither trained, nor prepared to handle what happened to me. He never asked me if I needed medical attention and, beyond the most rudimentary of psychological attentiveness on his part, he never referred me to any mental health professionals (much less inform the court or his superiors of the event) (Davies, 2002). His actions, while merit worthy also reveal an abject failure on the part of the Sherriff's Office to prepare correctional staff for these events, and illustrates in my case only an *ad hoc*, informal adaptation to this lack of training as I was left sitting in a swivel chair in the jury room with a Dixie cup of water and a view.

CONCLUSION

In this article, I intended to expose readers to a first-person, autoethnographic account "insider's account" of the complex dynamics of life within one medium security correctional facility in Southeastern Louisiana for a young, middle class, gay Latino male and my experience of sexual assault while temporarily housed there. I began with a brief discussion of the autoethnographic methods, combined with an application of "convict criminology" to elaborate upon my personal narrative. I then described the circumstances of my incarceration and the events in the lead-up to my assault. Next, I analyzed prison sexual culture, as well as the complexities of sex and sexuality within one correctional facility, and the discourses about prison rape that permeate popular culture and the public consciousness. I now conclude with a brief discussion about the politics of prison sexual assault and a summary of my personal reactions subsequent to my escape from my attacker and release from the institution.

Beth Richie (2012, p. 105) argues that the nature of a "prison nation" where neoliberal "law and order" authorities seek to "maintain the status quo *rather than* to prevent or remedy the range of social problems [like rape] associated with male violence for those [like gay men] who are most socially isolated, economically disadvantaged or politically powerless". Indeed, my experience occurred precisely within a criminal justice system more occupied with policing and stigmatizing sexual nonconformists, than with remedying any of the inattention to sexual victimization among LGBTQ prisoners.

Many gay men, lesbians and transgender prisoners are the most vulnerable among prison populations and are in desperate need of heightened safety measures when under the direct supervision, control, and bodily immobilization exercised upon them by state correctional institutions. The simple fact is that my escape was the product of my own initiative, the willingness of a staff member who happened to be in the right place at the right time and no small amount of luck. And, when I consider the failures of the criminal justice system to protect me, and the vulnerability of my queer brothers and sisters behind bars, I can only hope that recent advancements in political power *outside* correctional institutions will slowly change the circumstances of life for those LGBTQ prisoners *inside* them.

ENDNOTES

[1] I specifically use "gay" to denote the identity subject position, rather than the medico-psychological term of homosexual.

[2] The Eighth Amendment in the U.S. Constitution states: "Excessive bail shall not be required, nor excessive fines imposed, nor cruel and unusual punishments inflicted".

[3] Arkansas, Illinois, Massachusetts, North Carolina, New Hampshire, and Virginia.

[4] I never was able to determine who he was, but I *do* remember and I will never forget it or forgive him for his contribution to what happened to me.

REFERENCES

Adams, Tony E. and Stacy Holman Jones (2011) "Telling Stories: Reflexivity, Queer Theory, and Autoethnography", *Cultural Studies <--> Critical Methodologies*, 11(2): 108-116.

Anderson, Leon (2006) "Analytic Autoethnography", *Journal of Contemporary Ethnography*, 35(4): 373-395.

Castle, Tammy and Christopher Hensley (2002) "Argot Roles and Prison Sexual Hierarchy", in Christopher Hensley (ed.), *Prison Sex: Practice & Policy*, Boulder: Lynne Rienner Publishers, pp. 13-26.

Complete College America (2011) "2012 Remediation Report". Retrieved from State Data – Louisiana: <http://www.completecollege.org/docs/Louisiana.pdf>.

Crawford, Charles (2001) "Sexual Violence: Policies, Practices, and Challenges in the United States and Canada", in James F. Kelley (ed.), *Sexual Assault Behind Bars: The Forgotten Victims*, Santa Barbara: Praeger.

Davies, Michelle (2002) "Male Sexual Assault Victims: A Selective Review of the Literature and Implications for Support Services", *Aggression and Violent Behavior*, 7(3): 203-214.

Denzin, Norman (1997) *Interpretive Ethnography: Ethnographic Practices for the 21st Century*, London: Sage.

Ellis, Carolyn, Tony E. Adams, and Arthur P. Bochner (2011) "Autoethnography: An Overview", *Forum: Qualitative Social Research*, 12(1).

Farmer V. Brennan (1994) 511 U.S. 825, 834 United States Supreme Court.

Fleisher, Mark S. and Jessie L. Krienert (2009) *The Myth of Prison Rape: Sexual Culture in American Prisons,* Lanham: Rowman & Littlefield Publishers.

Gatson, Sarah N. (2003) "On Being Amorphous: Autoethnography, Genealogy, and Multiracial Identity", *Qualitative Inquiry*, 9(1): 28-48.

Heil, P., L. Harrison and K. English (2005) "Community Recidivism Rates of Institutional Sexual Offenders", presentation at the *24th Annual Research & Treatment Conference*, Salt Lake City: Association for the Treatment of Sexual Abusers.

King, Michael B. and Gillian C. Mezey (1992) *Male Victims of Sexual Assault*, Oxford: Oxford University Press.

Knowles, Gordon James (1999) "Male Prison Rape: A Search For Causation and Prevention", *The Howard Journal of Criminal Justice*, 39(3): 267-282.

Kunselman, Julie, Richard Tewksbury, Robert W. Dumond and Doris A. Dumond (2002) "Nonconsensual Sexual Behavior", in Christopher Hensley (ed.), *Prison Sex: Practice & Policy*, Boulder: Lynne Rienner Publishers, pp. 27-47.

Kunzel, Regina (2008) *Criminal Intimacy: Prison and the Uneven History of Modern American Sexuality,* Chicago: University of Chicago Press.

Mariner, Joanne (2003) "Deliberate Indifference", in Paul Wright and Tara Herivel (eds.), *Prison Nation: The Warehousing of America's Poor*, New York: Routledge, pp. 231-244.

Richie, Beth (2012) *Arrested Justice: Black Women, Violence and America's Prison Nation*, New York: New York University Press.

Ross, Jeffery Ian, and Stephen C. Richards (2009) *Beyond Bars: Rejoining Society After Prison*, New York: Alpha/Penguin Group.

Scacco, Anthony (1982) *Male Rape: A Casebook of Sexual Aggressions*, New York: AMS Press.

Tarzwell, Sydney (2006) "The Gender Lines Are Marked with Razor Wire: Addressing State Prison Policies and Practices for the Management of Transgender Prisoners", *Columbia Human Rights Law Review*, 38: 167-171.

Tewksbury, Richard (2007) "Effects of Sexual Assaults on Men: Physical, Mental and Sexual Consequences", *International Journal of Men's Health*, 6(1): 22-35.

Tewksbury, Richard, and Angel West (2000) "Research On Sex In Prison During the Late 1980s and Early 1990s", *The Prison Journal*, 80(4): 368-378.

Turner, Stuart (1992) "Surviving Sexual Assault and Sexual Torture", in Gillian C. Mezey (ed.), *Male Victims of Sexual Assault*, Oxford: Oxford University Press, pp. 75-85.

Wooden, Wayne S. and Jay Parker (1982) *Men Behind Bars: Sexual Exploitation in Prison*, New York: Plenum Press.

ABOUT THE AUTHOR

Michael Johnson Jr., PhD, is a full-time instructor in the Department of Critical Culture, Gender, and Race Studies at Washington State University, where he currently teaches both introductory and upper-division interdisciplinary undergraduate courses. His book, *Tickle My Fancy, Fat Man: Emerging Images of Race and Queer Desire on HBO*, is currently under contract with Lexington Press as part of its Critical Studies in Television Series (in press, fall 2015). His work can be found in the *Journal of Men's Studies*, *Reconstruction: Studies in Contemporary Culture*, *Journal of Prisoners on Prisons*, *Educational Studies*, and chapters in edited collections by ABC-Clio, Praeger, Palgrave Macmillan, Information Age Press and the University of New Mexico, to name a few.

We Are the Products of Our Experiences:
The Role Higher Education Plays in Prison

*Robert "Diesel" Shoemaker, Brandon "B" Willis
and Angela Bryant* *

INTRODUCTION

As of 2012, an estimated 2.2 million people were incarcerated in jails and prisons in the United States[1]. Prisoners are disproportionately likely to come from economically disadvantaged backgrounds, to be members of racial/ethnic minority groups, to have held a low-skill, low-paying job (if any at all) at the time of arrest, and to be less educated than their counterparts in the general population (Harlow, 2003). The problem is the most accessible trade available to the poor is crime. Once crime has been committed and the victims are served, criminals are put into very negative living situations leaving everyone with a question: does prison really change people? Of course it does because prison is an experience unparalleled to any other. Throughout the United States, the majority of people released from prison re-offend. People in prison are isolated from society, technology, and the experiences that are needed to change their lives. "There is a direct correlation between attainment and recidivism. Data suggest that better educated prisoners are less likely to relapse into criminal behavior after release from prison" (Erisman and Contardo, 2005, p. 5). If a person has an educational experience inside of prison, they are more likely to succeed in not coming back. Education leads to jobs and trades which help people step away from crime. Education in Ohio prisons is lacking because it is very limited. It is also restricted to only a select few. If something is good or proven to be effective, why limit it to only a few?

This paper reflects on life and prison experiences for Diesel and B (as well as other prisoners) that led to shifts in perceptions of the role of higher education in prison. The *Journal of Prisoners on Prisons* has dedicated special issues to the perils, pitfalls and benefits of higher education in prisons (see volumes 4(1), 13 and 17(1)). This article draws on the importance of higher education in prisons, but also adds a new dimension by drawing on the benefits of Inside-Out college courses in prison that include university students, requires the same course work, and provides college credit for both sets of students. Specifically, the article supports what Carter (2008) discusses as the importance of voluntary education in prisons as a conduit for liberating the mind and what Collins (2008) discusses as the importance of connecting education to marketable skills, rather than coerced fruitless education designed as another mechanism of control. Additionally, Beck, Richards and Elrod (2008) discuss the benefits of prison visitation for academics as a means of learning about the realities of prison life, but inside-out courses provide both academics and future criminal justice workers (outside students) weekly on-going exposure in numerous forms (e.g., formal meetings with prison officials to go over the rules of the institution, entering the prison weekly through differing security measures, observing staff/prisoner interactions, and class discussions with prisoners). Further, the Inside-out pedagogy dismantles much of what Collins (2008) and Huckelbury (2009) discuss as the tools prisons use to successfully separate, categorize and stigmatize the criminalized (see Garfinkel, 1956). The importance of linguistics is an ongoing discussion in inside-out courses in order to deconstruct what Huckelbury (2009, p. 27) finds as a primary function of prison, a "linguistic laboratory that identifies and perpetuates a specific social order".

This article seeks to demonstrate that experience and education are the most effective tools for change. If we leave penal policy as it stands, we will see no change for the overwhelming majority of men and women who are eventually returning to our communities. If we change our prison and education policies, we will see prisoners change. In this article, we address how our experiences shaped our understanding of the "fast life", our prison and educational experiences, as well as those of former and current prisoners, the glaring connections between education and recidivism, and possible solutions for penal education policies. Along with prisoners' views and experiences on each topic, we will demonstrate the possibilities for society and individuals by policies that have the capacity to turn a negative environment (prison) into a positive experience.

IS THE FAST LIFE LEARNED?

For many, the fast life is an attainable fairy tale. Everybody wants economic success and for the most disadvantaged in society this can lead people down a path of prison, addiction, and/or death. When you run as fast as you can, are you able to turn a sharp angle without first slowing down? Living without thinking about the turns can be very detrimental. To quote Jada Kiss' song: "The penitentiary chances that I take can get me the mansion by the lake". We are inundated with glorified versions of how we want to live through music and movies. The fast life is addictive on all levels: fast cars, money, women, drugs and so on. Jackboys (robbers) get addicted to the adrenaline. They tend to blow their money fast leaving them the choice to stop or rob again. Yet, they get addicted to the money and feeling of being on top of the world. They get their power through fear and money. We asked a few fellow prisoners their definitions of the fast life:

> Something that you get into where you're not responsible and not being a parent. Its dangerous and you never think of the consequences until it's too late. It takes over your conscience. It's living a dream that's not even real.

And,

> Something that you get into where you don't want true responsibility nor even care of its consequences. It takes over your conscience of thinking.

American capitalist culture teaches our young that success is judged by who has more, not by who they are. We see music videos showing the fast life of money, jewelry and beautiful women – the adult version of a fairy tale. Many people try to find shortcuts to success, leading to a path of destruction and mayhem. Today, living beyond one's means is the new epidemic. When one does not have the life they wanted, they become bitter so they begin concentrating on the jump and not the walk. We also asked fellow prisoners whether the fast life was worth it:

> No! I was not being a good father, son, brother. I distanced myself from my family. I became too busy for others acting like I cared for everyone but never showing it.

And,

> No! I felt like I was not being a good father to my kids, son to my parents and brother to my sisters and brothers. I became distant to my family.

We need to reexamine America's values. The United States makes up 5 percent of the world's population, yet houses 25 percent of the world's prisoners, spending an estimated $68 billion a year on corrections (Senator Jim Webb, 2009). It is no surprise why many chose to live the fast life given the lies we are told and the fairy tales we are taught are reality. We are taught accomplishments are won not earned. We look at the beginning and end of the story, not what happens in between. We walk around desensitized to the world around us causing and experiencing depression, another plague sweeping America. So, we ask as former drivers in the fast lane: Can we learn something else?

PERSONAL EXPERIENCE FOR B

When I first got locked up, my father came to visit me in the county jail. He told me to do something with my time and to get into college. He knew that being labelled a felon, from experience, can really alter the opportunities a person can have in life. I already felt my freedoms being restricted and stripped away from me every day in every way, from using the bathroom to using the telephone. After my sentencing, I finally felt the nervousness of what might happen to me go away. I had to do five years in Southeastern Correctional Complex (SCC), a medium/minimum prison camp.

I told myself I was going to use this time as a self-training camp, to get myself right physically, mentally, and make a plan to have a successful life once released. The plan of course was a legal plan. However, I had to find my way into college. Like everyone else, I had to deal with prison life. Nevertheless, there were requirements to get into college and stay in college. One of the main rules was not to miss more than one class a quarter, which ultimately meant I needed to stay out of 'the hole' (segregation). Also, you cannot have more than two Rule Infraction Board (R.I.B.) tickets. If those two rules were broken, I would be kicked out of college for a year. I already qualified for college because I had a high-school diploma.

My biggest problem was the selection of what was offered in college. I really wanted to learn more technical training with computers, but that option was not available. However, I knew that to survive and be successful once released, I would have to have an edge or advantage on the educational level. College has given me that edge. That opportunity should be offered to everyone, at least in some form. Not everyone wants to be in Landscaping or Business Management. A few of my friends told me that is why they did not join. Once I got in and started taking classes, I started to see how what I learned ties into the business world.

Prison life is very hard to deal with while being in school. You sometimes have to face the fact that you have to protect yourself and your possessions. That runs the risk of getting kicked out of college for a year. With a little luck, I managed to stay in college. Having a five-year sentence, in my fourth year I faced another problem; I was running out of classes to take because there are not that many courses offered. However, the college I have experienced has changed my life completely. The confidence you get from learning can be the difference in staying out or coming back.

PERSONAL EXPERIENCE FOR DIESEL

While sitting in the confines of one of the loneliest places man has ever known, I write. I write of experiences I had in prison and the perceptions that have changed during my ten plus years of incarceration. I, in turn, have seen this whole prison's mentality change. I have seen C.O.s get beat up and I have been victim of their beatings. I have been stabbed and have been in more fights than I can count. I have seen prisoners set up the C.O.s to lose their jobs and/or catch a case. On the other end of the spectrum, I have seen C.O.s set prisoners up from petty things to planting drugs on them so the prisoner gets more time. I have seen C.O.s bring stuff in and bring stuff out. I have been in the middle of riots and been an independent fighter hired to fight others. I have hustled with running a store and football tickets. I have seen and/or experienced a lot in the joint.

I started my bit like most do, in the County Jail. I knew then I was losing my identity. The deputies only called me by my last name and the prisoners called me young blood or youngster. They told me horror stories of prison and being an impressionable nineteen year old, I believed the words of my elders. They said you got to fight boy, fight. If you want to live and not be raped you can never lose. Strike fear into the convicts' hearts in order to survive. You must fight the biggest bad ass guy there and win. The judge struck his gavel and said thirteen years. I knew then I must push my humanity aside and send home the only thread that keeps anyone from being animals themselves – my conscience. I knew I must become an animal to survive in a concrete jungle full of animals. A place where the only way to come out whole is to eat or be eaten, attack or be attacked. I was sent to C.R.C., a reception center. C.R.C. is the place where you send home the clothes you wore on your last day free – your last reminder of who you used to be and will never be again. The new prisoners are stripped in front of everyone. No more dignity, no more humanity, just left in the chilly air as you stand there. I was 168 pounds and was told to bend over and spread them at intake. I resisted and fought the C.O. only to have many men in grey come to his aid and beat me down. I was thrown in a cell where the lights were always on, left alone to my torturous thoughts.

I was classed a level four security and sent to a closed, maximum security camp where they dropped me instantly to a level three in security. This place was called Ross Correctional Institute (R.C.I.), one of four maximum security prisons in Ohio where the hardest, toughest prisoners went. My thirteen-year sentence was considered short compared to the average sentence for "lifers". Before my cell door was open, I saw a monster of a man named "Big Franks". I fought him and won. There were many other fights and victories before everyone on the yard knew who I was. I was called "Diesel" at 168 pounds because of my intensity in everything I did. All the gang heads wanted to recruit me, but I told myself I was stronger than that and I would get through this as a lone wolf. I never lied in prison, nor did I go out my way to disrespect anyone. I only handled what turned up on my plate. For that, I gained the respect of lifers and the majority of prisoners. A former friend of mine lost a fight and was raped. He was moved over with me. I felt some humanity again by feeling bad for him. He walked as a hollow shell of the man he once was, in another world barely speaking anymore.

Eleven years to go in the midst of all the confusion prison brings, I saw a light of hope. I went to another's cell to see him doing college work. "What?", I said to myself, "the prison has college?!" I was filled with so much happiness and hope for my future. No longer would this be my life. Scarred up knuckles and bloody memories were a thing of the past. Then, I was told the criteria. I would have to wait until I had only five years left and eight years incarcerated. I argued, "don't they understand I could be out in eight years?" Once I served my three-year gun specification and five of my ten years left, I would be eligible for early release. I did some programs – some helped some did not. One day, three and a half years in, they dropped my security to a level two and sent me to Southeastern Correctional Complex (SCC). The prisoners called it gladiator school because at SCC, you fight for something to do, not to make it out alive. Fighting in SCC is entertainment to the general population because the average sentence is two years. My sentence was considered long at SCC. In my first fight at SCC I beat a man with the same intensity as I would have done at Ross. They almost gave me a new charge of assault until they realized what prison I came from. I realized then I had to lighten up and get some of my humanity back (conscience). I put that intensity into working out becoming big as a result. It took me another three years (six years into my sentence) to be able to talk to people, like people and not animals. I lost many family members, but in my seventh year I lost my close grandmother. I felt so much pain and loss that it made me human again. Comforted that I felt again, I took every opportunity I could only to be told there was a waiting list but I signed up for welding. Even though I did not have to wait until I was within five years of my release, it was worse because whoever is on the list and is closest to their release date gets accepted. In a prison where two years is the average sentence, guys like me may never get vocational training. We get out earlier with more time than the average ever does on a sentence. Ten years in and never accepted into welding because three years left on my sentence was still more than most at SCC.

Eight years into my sentence, I was excited to be accepted into college. Eight years of waiting for this moment and I was told of how limited it is. The college offered at SCC is freshman business courses and landscape courses, but I still enrolled to brighten my future. It may not have been what I pursue upon release, but it did broaden my horizons. It gave me the confidence that I can be anything I want to be in life through hard work and persistence. Continuing through failures, college showed me new directions in life. Earning all A's and making Deans list every quarter gave me confidence and hope of a better future. When we become enlightened what education can do, why are we limited to freshman levels in only one or two fields? I hungered as a scholar, but I had limited food a scholar needs to get its fill, education. In hindsight I now have the confidence to accomplish anything in life and know that because of college education I am hopeful that anything is attainable through hard work and direction.

LIMITED EDUCATION AND ITS STIPULATIONS

The college programs available in some of Ohio prisons are required by law to focus on advanced job training and no prisoner can obtain a degree. The highest course at SCC is freshman level. Communication classes are taken out of the curriculum to stop us from obtaining an associate's degree. SCC has small Business management, H.V.A.C. (Heating, Ventilation, Air Conditioning) and Landscape management courses. They used to have Hospitality courses too, but due to budget crunches it was removed. Each program is great. However, with roughly 1600 prisoners, not everyone wants to study in these fields, nor are they directly aligned with job opportunities in our communities. The few who are accepted into the limited seats available are only brought so far before they have no more to study.

To get into college in Ohio prisons you have to have less than five years left on your sentence, you cannot have more than two R.I.B. tickets, and you cannot have certain convictions (e.g. the majority of people with sex crime convictions are excluded from any type of college education). You must have a G.E.D. or high school diploma, you cannot have a college degree, and to stay enrolled, you cannot miss more than one class. G.E.D. programs are much more easily attainable in Ohio prisons because there are little criteria and almost no restrictions on who can be accepted.

Vocational programs and other programs like Substance Abuse and Anger management have a waiting list. The short timers get moved on the list before other prisoners with longer sentences are accepted. Some of these lists are majorly flawed because of how people are accepted according to one's maximum release date. Most people are sent to prison with plea agreements –agreements to get us to plead to guilty to the charges brought against us. If someone is sentenced to three years and promised early release after one year, that person will probably never be accepted into a vocational program because they are not close to their maximum sentence date, yet they will likely get out early. Vocational programming at SCC includes Drafting, Welding, Carpentry and Plumbing. Yet, on average, only 10 of 100 people can complete one of these programs – very limited seating for the countless incarcerated.

RECIDIVISM, EDUCATION AND THE CONNECTIONS

We have seen people come and go, in and out of these walls with new numbers or their old ones. We have collectively (not literally) seen 250,000 prison numbers pass through in our sentence time. Close to 95 percent of people who go to state prisons eventually get out[2]. College is a direction but why limit it? Few people take college at SCC because of it limited options of the courses offered and / or the criteria to get into it, and it is never enough to complete a full degree. Yet, a college degree would show employers upon release that you are worth the chance because you take interest in your own future. It was just a few years before we got locked up that Pell grants were repealed for prisoners, which meant they took out the bachelor's degrees and associates degrees in a variety of higher education areas. Our prison population in Ohio went from 31,862 in 1990 to 51,060 in 2009[3].

Being locked up, we have had conversations with other prisoners that we consider friends. We asked them why they did what they did. Most said crime was what they were taught or all they knew. Logically thinking, we need to be taught something else. Education enlightens us to better ways of life and teaches us how to financially support ourselves. A former prisoner states: "While incarcerated and attending college I learned a tremendous amount of things. One being organized and to take care of my responsibilities. When solving a problem, not to look at one way of solving, but several ways of doing so". He also stated: "Life isn't the same. I plan ahead now instead of rolling with the punches". He is currently enrolled in college and majoring in psychology.

The following quotes are some examples of current prisoner's views on education:

> Education has given me hope for a better start when I get released from prison; it gives me confidence to be able to do what needs to be done when I'm released. I will be able to support my family. That's why I feel it's going to help me in life.

And,

> Education for me has helped me grow and take more responsibilities in life. I found that I can believe in myself and become a success.

And,

> Educational training has changed my outlook on life by giving hope and possibly a new lease on life. My training can help me only if I pursue avenues in which my newly acquired knowledge and skills are relevant. This experience has helped me to exercise a better and more disciplined work ethic.

And,

> I was sentenced to ten years in prison. Part of my plea agreement was to get Judicial Release after five years (early release) for good behavior. The major thing about this is that if your out date is over five years then you are put on a waiting list. By the time I become eligible for the programs, it will be too late because you can be up for judicial release and you may not have any programs completed. That may stop you from being released. These are depressing concerns I have.

These men's statements show us we can to effectively reduce crime, the prison population and various other problems in our society by funding more educational programs. After all, most people who get locked up get out.

We have asked many prisoners who came back, why? They all in their own ways or words said the same thing – "I know nothing else". Yet, education in prison and the participants' statistics show success: re-arrest rates are 50%; re-conviction 26% and reincarceration 24% compared to those who did not receive or participate in educational programming whose re-arrests are 58%, re-conviction 33%, and reincarceration 31% (Steurer *et al.*, 2001). Furthermore, recent research in the state of Ohio disentangles the effects of college, high school, G.E.D., vocational training, and no education or the likelihood of returning to prison, for any reason up to 13.5 years past release and finds that college has the strongest impact on reducing recidivism rates (Batiuk *et al.*, 2005).

THE INSIDE-OUT PRISON EXCHANGE PROGRAM

> Though we postulate a sense of justice as a foundation of social life, there is much evidence to indicate that the public, lacking understanding

and interests in the causes of crime, still clings to the idea of individual responsibility (Clemmer, 1958, p. 318).

The Inside-Out Prison Exchange Program is an international initiative directed at transforming ways of thinking about crime and justice[4]. The idea for the program came from Paul Perry, a man serving a natural life sentence in Pennsylvania, and was established by Lori Pompa in 1997 to bring college students and incarcerated individuals together as peers in a classroom setting that emphasizes dialogue and critical thinking. In the hopes of expanding this innovative partnership between institutions of higher learning and prison systems nationally, Pompa organized the Inside-Out National Instructor Training Institute in 2004, with the assistance of the Philadelphia Prison System, Temple University and the Soros Foundation. To date, over 310 instructors from more than 150 colleges and universities in 37 states, two Canadian provinces and abroad have taken part in the Training Institute, returning to their universities and offering upwards of 300 classes across a range of disciplines[5]. As a result, Inside-Out has been able to bring over 10,000 "inside" (incarcerated) and "outside" (university) students together in classrooms behind prison walls.

The first two authors participated in the Inside-Out course that the third author offered at SCC in Autumn 2010. A few critical elements of the inside-out pedagogy are: the use of first names only; the ongoing conversations about the use of labeling language (e.g. use of obvious negative terms like "inmate", but also more subtle linguistic terms such as "us" or "them"); circles for all class discussions (alternating inside and outside students); students are required to actively participate each week; each participant's voice is equal, including the instructor whose role is as facilitator rather than expert lecturer; and, each class culminates with a group project designed to utilize empirical research to guide specific criminal justice policy recommendations, which is formally presented at a public closing ceremony[6]. Furthermore, it is made clear to the inside students that they are not only not expected to talk about what they are in for (e.g. convictions). The outside participants are not there to study those on the inside. We do not know what they are convicted of, as it is not our business and it is not relevant to what we are studying or the Inside-Out Prison experience. The goal of the course is to study issues, not people.

Our particular course content includes a series of critical readings and discussions focused upon such topics as the origins and development of the American criminal justice system, the historical and contemporary use of punishment and rehabilitation, the re-emergence of restorative justice, and the broader relationship between criminal and social justice. The course structure includes weekly three-hour sessions at the prison site. Enrollment includes 10-15 undergraduate university students and 10-15 incarcerated students. All course participants write a minimum of six reflection papers. The papers require that the students observe, reflect, analyze, and integrate the information in the readings with the prior week's discussion. In lieu of a final exam, a final paper of approximately ten pages in length is also required. The final paper is an opportunity for students to pull together the entire experience of the quarter, reflect on their own process (and that of the group), and further analyze the issues that were addressed.

Similar to previous research on the impact of higher education on prisoners (Torre and Fine 2005), Diesel and B describe perceptual shifts amongst inside student participants from seeing themselves as passive objects into seeing themselves as active subjects. They develop a sense of critical, personal agency, and an active, collective responsibility. To date, there are two specific published evaluations of Inside-Out courses that also support our perspectives of Inside-Out (see Davis and Roswell, 2013). Allred (2009) conducted a survey and an analysis of her Inside-Out students' reflection papers focused on one particular week's topic (what are prisons for) in order to determine how students ranked the importance of the structure of the class (icebreakers, large group brainstorming activities, and small group activities), the content of those class discussions, and the readings for that week. She found that students learned most from the course structure (followed by content and readings) because it created the interactions for students to shift their ideas about the topic and one another (2009). Second, Allred and colleagues (2013) conducted a pre/post General Self-efficacy Scale (Schwarzer and Jerusalem, 1995) survey across three different Inside-out courses. Not surprisingly, given the lower levels of educational attainment amongst prisoners, on the pre-course scale, outside students had significantly higher levels of general self-efficacy than inside students (Allred *et al.*, 2013). On the other hand, at post-course administration of the survey, only the inside students experienced a significant increase in self-efficacy (ibid). The study lends support to the importance of the Inside-Out pedagogy in that this study was implemented with different course content, at different prisons and with three different trained instructors, yet finds similar results.

It is important to note that when developing this course, the third author had university colleagues question the benefit of teaching a corrections class with prisoners. The assumption that was explicitly stated was that people in prison have obviously been directly impacted by corrections and therefore likely have the knowledge base. Of course, this is an erroneous assumption given that prisoners have had their individual subjective experiences in the system, but that does not equate to them necessarily having a full picture of the historical and contemporary issues prominent in corrections literature. In fact, often throughout the course, inside students commented about how little they knew about why things happened the way they did in their particular cases and many described moments of clarity after reading course material and discussing it in class in terms of understanding the context of the decisions that were made (see Mishne *et al.,* 2012). For most inside students, this course is likely the first prison educational experience where they had a voice, that their informed opinions mattered, and that they could have educational conversations with outside people who were not either family, nor worked in the system. It is likely the context of holding class inside the prison walls, the pedagogy of equal voices, and the interactions with each other as classmates shift participants' perceptions of themselves, others and the criminal justice system. Of particular relevance, the theme of recognizing every person's value as a human being is found in all five courses the third author has taught, as well as the realization that the prison system's method of depersonalization (e.g. the identification of prisoners by either their prison number or last name) allows most members of society to forget this basic fact. The pedagogy and context of Inside-Out courses serves as a mechanism to erode structural barriers – physical and emotional – between "us" and "them".

It is tragic that Pell Grants have yet to be reinstated for incarcerated men and women, as well as disappointing that many Inside-Out incarcerated students across the country do not earn college credits for their participation. SCC students are offered college credit for the course. According to the Ohio State University – Newark Dean MacDonald (Summer, 2011, National Inside-Out Prison Exchange Program newsletter, p. 4):

In a short time frame, Angela obtained internal and external grant funds to ensure the program's initial success and achieve permanent course-offering status. At the same time, she worked to ensure that both 'inside' and 'outside' participants who successfully completed her rigorous course achieved the same result: college credit. For her second course, she took interested 'inside' students through the university's admissions process and inspired our campus to utilize non-state-subsidized funds to support tuition costs for 'inside' students. But, she didn't stop there. Over the last year, she navigated multiple university offices and campuses to gain support from numerous decision-makers to make college credit and tuition for 'inside' students an enduring reality. The foundation of our rationale for doing so is that, without the incarcerated students' participation in the course, we would not be able to offer this unique experiential learning opportunity.

And, according to Warden Duffey at SCC (ibid):

Though cautious of such a different approach to learning for a correctional environment, this was an offer that appealed to me. Not only did the 'inside' students have a chance to participate in a course from a respected university, but they would be interacting with 'outside' students in a true learning environment...the excitement from the 'inside' students is easily seen. Word travels fast within the confines of the fence and the 'inside' students have heard they will be challenged each week. When they finish this course, they will have pride for completing such a demanding criminal justice class, and they will have a college credit. The 'inside' students were willing to participate in this course for the educational experience. They were not expecting to be able to obtain a college credit. This bonus adds to the positive reentry for 'inside' students to one day become 'outside' students. I have been pleasantly surprised to see the ownership taken by the offenders. They strive to comply with prison rules and maintain a positive attitude. Their self-confidence grows week to week as they feel like 'real' students. It has become the norm for the 'inside' students to speak about furthering their education upon their release. The Inside-Out program is more than a college class; it has become a vital step in the rehabilitative process, changing values and trends.

OUR INSIDE-OUT EXPERIENCE:
B AND DIESEL

Higher education changed our experiences from sitting in ignorance to embracing our lives, responsibilities and dreams. One of the most enlightening educational experiences we have had was the Inside-Out course we both completed in Autumn 2010. More people should have the Inside-Out experience – it is amazing to see what an inspirational professor can do. By showing through examples of perseverance and encouragement, students are pushed further. We were shown we could do more than just waste our time in prison. Programs like the Inside-Out Prison Exchange Program are needed in all prisons to inspire true change.

Starting the inside-out class in 2010, we never thought we would see in writing what we had felt over the long years of our incarceration. Everyone convicted is sentenced to life in one form or the other – a lifetime of roadblocks and "invisible" punishments not stated at sentencing (Mauer and Chesney-Lind, 2002). No longer are we judged by who we are and what we can achieve, but rather where we have been and we are from. Our skin is stained "blue" and we are permanently segregated by where we can work and live as convicted felons. The class showed us that we have all (not just those of us incarcerated) have been hurt by others and regretfully, hurt someone else. To quote some of our inside classmates:

> Inside-Out has changed the way I view my incarceration. It has shown me not to become a bitter man but a better man.

And,

> The thing that affected me most in the class is how many people are victims of crime. Not only did it hurt my heart that I added to these statistics, but it opened my eyes to how I can change and help others in my situation. I guess higher education goes hand in hand with rehabilitation.

And,

> Inside-out was an opportunity to see other people's perspectives other than mine on the criminal justice system. It made me realize that I am

not the only one who saw the problems. The course was something that
I learned to love and look forward to each week. The realization of us all
being equal for a short period of time was the most important aspect.

We all came to realize that because of the hurt we caused, our skin is stained
blue and we are cursed for it, but blessed because of it. At the heart of Inside-
Out is the realization that we are all just people – people who have hurt and
been hurt, people who laugh, cry, mourn, and struggle. The class let us rest
easier knowing there are actually people who care, people who recognize
what us "blue" are experiencing, and people who are really trying to change
the system. To say Inside-Out meant a lot to us would be an understatement.
It is life changing…'is' because we are still growing from the experience.
We took that class to be able to broaden the 'outside' students' perceptions,
and to learn more about criminal justice other than what we experienced.
Little did we know that it would be our perceptions that were blown out of
the water. We learned so many life lessons alongside the course readings.
After a disagreement in class, we realized how we came across to people,
even though it was not intentional. We learned it is not how you perceive
what you are saying, it is how others perceive it. It taught us not to let
prison conquer us into believing this is the only way of life. We learned
how to shape a better future, surrounding ourselves with the right people
and continuing education.[7]

ADDING AND DIVERSIFYING EDUCATION OPPORTUNITIES IN PRISON

With the success of higher education on reducing recidivism, why not
diversify education and make it for prisoners? If we did, fewer people would
come back. Utilizing research by Steurer and colleagues (2001), if 200,000
prisoners were educated, we would only see 48,000 (24%) come back to
prison. That is 152,000 staying out with their kids in their own family and/
or community. That is 152,000 ex-prisoners showing kids in the community
new and better ways to live. Not only does reincarceration drop dramatically
by educating prisoners, but future crime will drop because misled children
will be led differently and influenced to make better decisions. Diversifying
education opportunities will create less crime, which means fewer victims
and fewer prisons. This ultimately means less tax payer money being spent

on warehousing prisoners. It means less money spent on task forces. It means more people contributing. It is common knowledge that being locked up reduces one's chances at job opportunities upon release. It can be hard for people without a prison number to get a job without a college education. We know that in order for us to maintain and survive in the world outside of prison, we would essentially have to know more than we did and work harder than the average person.

Offering online courses would greatly help the deficiencies prisoners face today. The internet offers countless opportunities for education, yet it is banned in most prisons. A teacher could use a computer as a monitoring device to facilitate internet-based courses in prison and ensure prisoners' access was limited to the course only. Additionally, teachers could have the ability to copy assignments and other materials from the web and download them directly to students' computers without allowing direct access to the internet. Indirect access to the internet would diversify the college courses offered in prison and provide the necessary educational experiences for prisoners to be successful upon release.

If incarcerated people are enrolled in educational programs, it will give them a chance to learn how to function in society better. It will teach us the skills we need to obtain a higher paying job. Most of all, it will end the excuse of "this is all I know". Reinstating Pell grants to provide post-secondary education in prisons would change prison experiences, making prison a place of active learning, rather than a place to sit and wait until your released. We have personally experienced how educational opportunities can change an individual. Experiences and education are intertwined – one cannot exist without the other. There are great outcomes for prisoners who participate in postsecondary education, but as technology changes, curriculum should also be updated like it was in our Inside-Out course. In a few of our prison-based college courses, we use books that "Father Time" used. How are such outdated materials going to help prisoners? The longer the sentence served, the greater the disadvantages are for understanding technological developments. Punishing people for crime by banning us from society is one thing; crippling our knowledge by keeping us ignorant is another that serves no one, especially the communities we will re-join. We have learned if you have a desire to change you can, but only if you can obtain the knowledge you need to change.

TRUE CHANGE FOR DIESEL

While there were many reasons for personal change, there is no light switch that can be magically switched. Like the majority of prisoners, I did not automatically change because I was sentenced to prison. I wanted change so much that I thought I did change, but I was lacking the tools to actually change. When you are ignorant to new ways of living, you try but never accomplish much. Some great programs at SCC like Victims Awareness and Anger Management are designed to push you in a new direction, but it really is just a first step. After this first step, you wonder around mindlessly for a while you may move forward or backward or even further back than you were. The desire to change is definitely necessary and the majority of prisoners have this desire, but need much more than the first step to make change a reality. Higher education shows you the means to pursue a different life.

Almost everyone who has lost their freedom desires change, so how does throwing them in a stagnant place help? As an example, unripened fruit has not realized its potential. When it falls, it may bruise another piece of fruit on its way down to the ground. The caretakers pick up the unripened fruit and throw it in a box with the other bruised rotting fruit, where it starts to rot faster. If someone removes the piece of fruit, the rotting slows, but does not stop. It takes animals (programs) to eat the rotting flesh away and someone (education) has to take that seed and plant it. If provided the appropriate nutrients, the seed becomes a mighty tree that produces its own fruit.

Personally, prison was reason enough for me to want to change because of the hurt I caused and the place I landed. I came to realize that I lived my life in a repetitive circle – I would do good, then bad, then real good, then real bad, over and over again. Even though situations, places and people changed, the circle of my actions did not. I was a defiant person who was rebellious at heart. I lived selfishly with my own will and in turn, lost almost half of my life. My entire life I kept waiting for something to change, ignorant to actually making the change myself. When you want a car and do not have the resources to know how to get one, how do you go about getting a car? You do not unless you are educated on how to obtain the means to get a loan to purchase a car. I kept wondering why things kept happening to me, playing a victim when I was only a victim because of my own actions. I have lost many loved ones over the years and each experience made me never want to be in prison again. It is the same process for people in the free world. If I would not have made that decision, this and that would not have happened. We all participate in the "what if and could have been" conversations with ourselves.

When I lost one of the most significant people in my life, my grandmother, I was asked to be a pallbearer, something I never expected given the harms I have caused my family. I could not fulfill this request because of being incarcerated. I started to change because of this significant loss, but also because I was now finally eligible for college education in prison. I put everything I had into the first quarter even though throughout primary education I had received poor grades. With all my efforts (something I never put into primary education), I earned all A's and quickly learned that hard work and persistence pay off in achievements. Instructors told me that I was an above average student, an over-achiever, and a reminder of why they chose to teach to feed the hunger I had for knowledge. The more I learned, the hungrier I became for knowledge. People on the yard even started asking me what was different about me. I did not know then, but realize now it was the confidence in my walk, confidence that I am learning so much more about myself than the text.

Then, I took the Inside-Out course. It was life changing, a real eye opener. To write about all the things the course offered is another article. The class made me come to an understanding that truly challenged everything I had ever believed in and previously thought; that actions will always follow your beliefs and thoughts. It broadened my perceptions so much that I can never be the same person because of all the monumental changes I went through during the course. I changed my perceptions of everyone and they changed their perceptions of me. I realized I came off to people as very assertive (perhaps even aggressive) and I thought I was not judgmental, but quickly realized I was. One exercise we did in the class showed us that there may be "rights' and "wrongs", but not hard facts on who was right or what wrong took place. I was voted to have the honour of giving the speech at the public closing ceremony. When people heard what I said, many audience members teared-up and prison officials even rushed over to shake my hand and tell me that I had changed their perception of "inmates" forever. The media asked me for a copy of my speech to print and I observed heart-filled moments from everyone that day. I have never been more proud of who I was until that day. Everyone in that class will never forget the three months we learned from one another. I learned more from that class than what we ever discussed from the readings. I learned that there is no limit to one's life potential. There is no measuring tape in life that states you can only go this far. I realized that when a person sets a limit for themselves in life that is all the further they will go. I realized that if you keep putting yourself out there, eventually people notice. I have become a different man with the assistance of higher education. I now have the tools for how to live as a helping hand to society rather than a taker from society. Without education, change is impossible. You can have all the want for change in the world, but you have to learn a different way in order to walk one.

To me, change is changing the "what ifs" to "what will be" by learning how. Persistence in the right things leads to good outcomes. I learned what true ambition is and I now apply it to everything I do. Rather than waiting for something to happen and becoming stagnant, I pursue educational opportunities and become enriched. The courses I take make me more confident in life. I do not know the turns in the road ahead of me, but I do believe I can cross over any struggle because I have learned how. Knowledge makes me feel like a kid on Christmas morning waiting to unwrap more mysterious gifts that are still unknown. Enlighten the people of better turns and show them they can make the turn, and they will. My life was a turn of losses, but now I know how to achieve and have gained the ability to help others and so much more. True change is through education.

TRUE CHANGE FOR B

Change can only occur when that person wants to change. For better or worse, it is up to the individual. For me, I am trying my hardest to change for the better in order to set an example for my family. I want to show my family that even if you make a mistake (crime), you can turn your life around. Secondly, I want to prove to myself that I am not a failure and that I can control my own life. An old wise saying is that "knowledge is power" and I believe that to be true. If you cannot read or write, there is no opportunity for legal employment. In addition to reading and writing, college is a tool to obtain more power over how to live your life. The more you learn about something, the better you can become at that trade. College has provided me an environment where I can learn what I feel I need to succeed. College also provides me with a documented statement that I am trying. I can send home certificates to my family to let them know I am not just sitting in prison. Life is what we make of it and if we do not try and learn how to change, we will not change.

When taking the Inside-Out course, I noticed that one class changed me greatly. We were able to discuss and hear how others view crime and ethics. What really hit me was a victimization survey we did in class because it revealed that the happy people sitting beside me had been through a lot in their lives. Every person was either directly victimized by crime or had a loved one victimized. This information put faces on statistics. Now, every time I read a statistic like, "this state has an average of 50% recidivism" or "1 out of every 10 households has a woman who has been sexually assaulted", I think of those faces. I think of my sister, niece, mother, neighbours and friends and, for the first time, can put myself in their shoes. It also saddened me to know I added to those statistics. Honestly, I looked at myself differently after that class.

Studying the effects of prison on family members was also a big eye opener for me. I know it is stressful on prisoners being locked up, but it is probably worse for our families. Trying to stay in touch with loved ones in prison can be quite expensive. My own family drives over two hours to visit me to show their support, which I must admit is a big hit to my male ego because of feeling like a child again who needs the love and support of their family. I learned how stressful it can be on a family to have the breadwinner, father/mother, husband/wife incarcerated. In part, this is why it is so natural to be on edge in prison. I started understanding how people felt and in the end, started treating people better. Taking the Inside-Out class taught me to be more empathetic to people's views, opinions and situations. That may not have been in the course syllabus, but some of the best lessons learned can be just inside of an experience alone. I had a wonderful teacher who pushed me to do my best and I met some amazing people along the way. In fact, without that class and experience, I would not be writing this article today.

CONCLUSION

While there are good reasons to question a full restoration of rehabilitation, there are reasons to look there. One is that while modern rehabilitative correctionalism drew on many ideas from the UK and from Europe, it had strong American roots in its optimism about science and technology and about personal transformation. Much of the same optimism has helped to fuel mass incarceration on the promise that the warehouse prison could bring down crime by incapacitating criminals (Simon, 2010, p. 269).

As it has been proven over the centuries, history repeats itself over and over again unless change is implemented. While the illusion of a crime free world is a farce, methods for evaluating reducing crime need consistently re-evaluated in order to change as the world changes. Too often we have people in positions of power who seem to build their careers on being "tough on crime". While we are not questioning the need for punishment, it is the rehabilitation of the criminalized that the public is greatly misinformed about. Prison officials build smoke screens for the public with numbers, such as the numbers of prisoners per education class and the numbers of hours spent in the classroom. This information is presented to the public to instill a false sense of security and relinquish any feelings of societal responsibility. What the public does not know is just how behind the times correctional education is. Many people may argue that criminals do not deserve an education or any help whatsoever, but what they fail to acknowledge is the glaring fact that 95 percent of us are coming back to society, whose members need to decide whether they want ex-prisoners to be prepared to be a productive member of society or simply become another burden to society again. Higher education holds the most promise to reducing recidivism and in order to prepare people, this education must use current materials and technology. One cannot deny that utilizing course materials and technology that is over 14 years old in prison is viewed as acceptable because we are viewed as sub-par human beings. Former prisoners are already at a huge disadvantage when attempting to re-enter the workforce without adding fuel to the fire of a less than adequate education. Even worse, we are lead to believe that the education provided to us in prison is adequate for the workforce.

Statistics show that education is the key for the young not to go and the older to stay out of prison. Why do we ignore what we know for sure? It is time for us to stop focusing on the problem and start looking at the answer. Overall, knowledge leads to making the right experiences. Knowledge is the key for one to take control of their own life. With that said, we believe that diversifying the educational programs in prison will help reduce crime and give people what is most important – hope for a better life. This creates less victims and more positive influences in communities. Indirect internet-based courses can diversify course offerings in prison and allow more fields of study people would actually want to pursue upon release. Methods of course instruction and course materials can stay current without adding additional costs to the budget, such as Inside-Out courses. While we recognize the amazing growth of the Inside-Out program over the last ten years, we believe more universities and prisons should partner to utilize this pedagogy because it is beneficial for all involved. We also believe that current Inside-Out universities should offer more series-based courses in order to allow all students, but particularly incarcerated students, to continue down the educational path.

We are all guilty of acting first without thinking because it is so easy to wash your hands of the outcomes when you believe you are not directly involved or impacted. As a society, we are all involved in the Prison Industrial Complex no matter what lies we tell ourselves to sleep better at night. It is time we take a hard honest look at the current penal system for what it is – a failure. Education is transformative and needed to change the failing correctional system. We are after all products of our experiences.

ENDNOTES

[*]   Numerous scholars provided very helpful feedback on earlier drafts of this paper: Hal Pepinsky (Professor Emeritus, Indiana University), Michael J. Coyle (Associate Professor, California State University-Chico) and Dylan Adams (B.A., The Ohio State University). Also, we must acknowledge prison administrators at Southeastern Correctional Complex (SCC) for allowing Dr. Bryant to work with us on this article. This article started in SCC, but we finished it after Diesel and B were released.

[1]   See <http://www.sentencingproject.org/template/page.cfm?id=107>.

[2]   See <http://www.nationalreentryresourcecenter.org/facts>.

[3]   See <http://www.lsc.state.oh.us/fiscal/ohiofacts/sep2010/justiceandpublicsafetysystems.pdf>

[4]   For a comprehensive overview of Inside-Out see Davis and Roswell (2013).

[5]   For more information see <http://www.insideoutcenter.org/>.

[6]   For a discussion of some of the problems with some of the parameters and rules of Inside-Out see VanGundy, Bryant and Starks (2013).

[7]   See Mishne and colleagues (2012) for a further discussion of what both inside and outside students gain.

REFERENCES

Allred, Sarah L. (2009) "The Inside-Out Prison Exchange Program: The Impact of Structure, Content, and Readings", *The Journal of Correctional Education*, 60(3): 240-258.

Allred, Sarah L., Lana D. Harrison and Daniel J. O'Connell (2013) "Self-efficacy: An Important Aspect of Prison-based Learning", *Prison Journal,* 93(2): 211-233.

Batiuk, Mary Ellen, Karen F. Lahm, Matthew McKeever, Norma Wilcox and Pamela Wilcox (2005) "Disentangling the Effects of Correctional Education: Are Current Policies Misguided? An Event History Analysis", *Criminal Justice,* 5(1): 55-74.

Beck, Victoria Simpson, Stephen C. Richards and Preston Elrod (2008) "Prison Visits: On the Outside Looking In", *Journal of Prisoners on Prisons,* 17(1): 91-105.

Carter, Rod (2008) "My Experience with Education in Canada and Federal Prisons", *Journal of Prisoners on Prisons,* 17(1): 61-70.

Clemmer, Donald (1958) *The Prison Community,* New York: Rinehart & Company Inc.

Collins, Peter (2008) "Education in Prison or The Applied Art of 'Correctional' Deconstructive Learning", *Journal of Prisoners on Prisons,* 17(1): 71-90.

Davis, Simone and Barbara S. Roswell (eds.) (2013) *Turning Teaching Inside Out: A Pedagogy of Transformation for Community-Based Education,* New York City: Palgrave Macmillan.

Erisman, Wendy and Jeanne Bayer Contardo (2005) "Learning to Reduce Recidivism: A 50-state Analysis of Postsecondary Correctional Education Policy", Washington, DC: The Institute for Higher Education Policy – November. Retrieved from: <http://www.ihep.org/Publications/publicationsdetail.cfm?id=47>.

Garfinkel, Harold (1956) "Conditions of Successful Degradation Ceremonies", *American Journal of Sociology,* 61(5): 420-424.

Harlow, Caroline Wolf (2003) "Education and Correctional Populations", U.S. Department of Justice, Office of Justice Programs Bureau of Justice Statistics Special Report – January. Retrieved from: <http://bjs.gov/content/pub/pdf/ecp.pdf>.

Huckelbury, Charles (2009) "Talking Points: How Language Functions as a Status Determinant in Prison", *Journal of Prisoners on Prisons,* 18(1&2): 22-28.

Mauer, Marc and Meda Chesney-Lind (eds.) (2002) *Invisible Punishment: The Collateral Consequences of Mass Imprisonment,* New York: New Press.

Mishne, Laura, Erica Warner, Brandon Willis and Robert Shomaker (2012) "Breaking Down Barriers: Student Experiences of the Inside-Out Prison Exchange Program", *Undergraduate Journal of Service Learning and Community-Based Research,* Penn State-Berks: 1-14.

Senator Jim Webb (2009) "What's Wrong with our Prisons?", *Parade Magazine* – March 29.

Simon, Jonathon (2010) " Do These Prisons Make Me Look Fat? Moderating the USA's Consumption of Punishment", *Theoretical Criminology,* 14(3): 257–272.

Steurer, Stephen J., Linda J. Smith and Alice Tracy (2001) *Three State Recidivism Study,* Landham (MD): Correctional Education Association.

The National Inside-Out Center Newsletter (2011) 2(2). Retrieved from: <http://www.insideoutcenter.org/PDF_newsletters/IO_Summer2011Newsletter_Color.pdf>.

Torre, María Elena and Michelle Fine (2005) "Bar None: Extending Affirmative Action to Higher Education in Prison", *Journal of Social Issues,* 61(3): 569-594.

Van Gundy, Alana, Angela Bryant and Brian C. Starks (2013) "Pushing the Envelope for Evolution and Social Change: Critical Challenges for Teaching Inside-Out", *Prison Journal,* 93(2): 189-210.

ABOUT THE AUTHORS

Robert "Diesel" Shomaker was incarcerated in Ohio prisons from 2001-2012. During his incarceration at SCC, he attended Hocking Community College for business management and landscape management and held a 4.0 GPA. Following his release, he has worked as a full-time employee at a steel factory and started his own landscape company, Plum Creek. Since 2012, he talks to troubled teens through a program at the Hebron New Life Methodist Church. He is currently working with his church and the local probation department to start a program for returning prisoners. He also serves as an invited guest lecturer at Ohio universities and Inside-Out regional meetings to discuss the barriers ex-prisoners face upon release. He has co-authored a paper with Brandon and two former outside students on the Inside-Out experience (see Mishne *et al.*, 2012).

Brandon "B" Willis was incarcerated at SCC from 2007-2012 for felonious assault. During his incarceration, he attended Hocking Community College for business management and landscape management and held a 3.8 GPA. Since his release, he has been employed as a foreman for a landscape company where he leads work crews for new home installation design in the Cincinnati, Ohio area. He also trains and competes in martial arts, as well as pursues his hip hop music. He also serves as an invited guest lecturer at Ohio universities and Inside-Out regional meetings to discuss the barriers ex-prisoners face upon release. He has co-authored a paper with Diesel and two former outside students on the Inside-Out experience (see Mishne *et al.*, 2012).

Angela Bryant is an Assistant Professor of Sociology, Ohio State University – Newark. Her research focuses on the organizational contexts of juvenile/ criminal courts, racial/ethnic, gender, and class disparities in case processing decisions, and the implementation and consequences of formal/ informal crime control policies and programs for juveniles and young adults in conflict with the law. She has been offering Inside-Out courses at Southeastern Correctional Complex since 2009.

Risk Assessment in New Zealand Prisons: Questioning Experiential Outcomes
Daniel Luff and Greg Newbold

INTRODUCTION

In spite of well-publicized drops in crime recorded in New Zealand over the past 20 years, prison populations have burgeoned. Since 1990, the New Zealand prison population has more than doubled, to a current muster of 8500. A great deal of the growth has been due to rises in violent crime prior to the early 1990s, harsher penalties for individuals convicted of violent offenses, and hair-trigger recall (i.e. parole violation for minor breaches) procedures (Newbold, 2007). As a result, the percentage of people in prison for violent offenses increased from 43 percent in 1987, to around 60 percent today (Newbold, 2007). Approximately 50 percent of all released prisoners are re-incarcerated within five years of release (Spier, 2007).

Because of the high levels of public concern about violent offending, significant research has gone into the development and implementation of various forms of violence risk assessment. Violence risk assessment in New Zealand prisons is used to determine a prisoner's security level, as well as to predict his/her readiness for release. This is important, because under the *Parole Act 2002* a prisoner in New Zealand cannot be released on parole unless the parole board adjudges him/her not to present an undue risk to the safety of the community. Prisoners with low security classifications have greater access to programs and are thus more likely to impress the parole board with their readiness for release. The purpose of this paper is to examine the risk assessment process in use in New Zealand prisons and to consider the reliability of its outcomes.

THE PROCESS OF RISK ASSESSMENT

Violence risk assessment has one fundamental purpose: to obtain some idea of an individual's likelihood of behaving violently in the future. Internationally, risk assessment is used in a wide range of settings (Shipley and Arrigo, 2012, p. 38). It is utilized most heavily, however, within government departments such as those of mental health and corrections. Within these sectors, hospital patients and prisoners are often assessed for risk of violence when decisions are being made about transfer to less secure facilities or whether to grant them release. In New Zealand, all prisoners who are incarcerated for violent offenses are assessed by either a Corrections Department or a Probation Service psychologist prior to their appearance before a parole board (Brady, 2009, pp. 2.6-2.7). A significant component of that assessment is a risk of violence evaluation (Brady, 2009, pp. 2.7, 2.9). The outcome of this evaluation becomes pivotal to the parole board's decision regarding transfer, or release and subsequent management (Petersilia, 2003, p.71).

The process of risk assessment has altered considerably over the years. During the 1970s and 1980s, risk assessment was comprised primarily of clinical judgment, a process that involved an expert professional considering all known factors about a subject – such as family background, educational level and offending history (Langan, 2010). On the basis of these factors, as well as a criminalized individual's personal presentation and demeanor, the clinical expert would, using their knowledge and experience, make an informed estimate of his/her level of risk. The range of factors to be considered was extensive, however, and this was one reason for the decline of the clinical approach. It was argued that there are too many circumstantial factors for an evaluator to be able to consider subjectively (Large and Nielssen, 2011, p. 414). The clinical method, although defended by its advocates on the basis that it treats a subject as an individual, has also been strongly criticized because subjective, clinical findings lack transparency and are prone to bias (ibid, p. 417).

It was largely due to such concerns about subjectivity that an actuarial approach to violence risk assessment was sought during the 1990s. Actuarial methods, which are applied within the New Zealand Department of Corrections today, involve the use of statistically-normed measurement tools. These tools, such as the Violence Risk Assessment Guide (VRAG), incorporate interval level scales that assess a set of factors that are held to be reliable predictors of violence (ibid, pp. 414-415). These factors include age, race, violence history and gender (Petersilia, 2003, p. 152). Depending on the number of predictors found, the subject of the assessment will obtain a score that designates him/her as either in a high or low risk category of future violence (Large and Nielssen, 2011, p. 415). The call for objectivity and the consequent mainstreaming of the actuarial model of assessment has largely sidelined the subjective clinical approach (Szmukler and Rose, 2013, p. 132). Clearly, the pertinent question in all of this is whether or not such developments have been more effective in predicting the risk of future violence. If the answer is no, then what are the implications and who is affected?

RISK ASSESSMENT AND OUTCOMES

The efficacy of actuarial risk assessment tools is the subject of controversy. A solid body of research supports the contention that actuarial instruments consistently produce more accurate findings than do clinical judgments (Langan, 2010, p. 90; Shipley and Arrigo, 2012, p. 36; Bakker *et al.* cited in Coombes and Te Hiwi, 2007, p. 383). However, others argue that the use of objective statistical tools has made no noteworthy addition to the struggle to accurately predict violence (Szmukler and Rose, 2013, p. 128). Another prominent argument is that hence, all currently-used forms of risk assessment, be they clinical, actuarial or a combination of both, can be wildly inaccurate (Large and Nielssen, 2011, pp. 414, 417). In fact, some consider that, given the difficulties involved, it is futile even to attempt to measure violence risk (Langan, 2010, p. 97).

One problem with statistical-based predictions of this type is that the personal and subjective circumstances of an individual cannot be taken into account and are often overlooked. Another problem is that due to the angry public reaction that sometimes follows an erroneous prediction, psychologists and parole authorities have learned to be cautious in their assessment procedures and interpretation. If a parolee offends seriously after an erroneous assessment, the decision makers cannot only face public pillorying, but also feel a grievous sense of personal responsibility for the outcome. A recent tragic example is that of Christy Marceau (age 18), who was stabbed to death at home in front of her mother in 2011. Her killer had been granted bail on charges of kidnapping, threatening and assaulting Christie only four weeks before, and had been bailed to an address near her. The case caused massive public outrage and withering criticism of the judge concerned. Whilst opinions on the issue are diverse, Shipley and Arrigo (2012, p. 42) sum up the various arguments by noting that, at present, none of the existing risk assessment tools are able to give highly accurate predictions of future risk. "Our field's ability to accurately predict who will engage in future violence is still limited", they write (ibid, p. 35). Thus, whilst those tools may arguably be more accurate than clinical prediction, much remains unclear, or at least unproven, regarding their usefulness to the assessment process. What is clear, however, is that the accuracy of actuarial instruments is overestimated by those who use them. Another thing that is apparent is that violence risk assessment, in its present form, produces a number of unjust outcomes, which we outline below.

THE CONSEQUENCES OF FALSE-POSITIVES

While risk-averse policies may reduce the minority of cases where tragic consequences follow, they also have the converse effect of keeping individuals in confinement who in fact present no real threat to the community. Such an outcome, known as a false positive, is unfair to individuals and damages the credibility of the system. Although legal authorities usually justify a high number of false positives through the claim that they serve "the wider good" (Large and Nielssen, 2011, p. 416), false positives can also negatively impact on the mental health and reformative progress of a criminalized person.

Being classified as having a high risk of future violence – erroneously or not - has a number of negative effects. A prisoner who is assessed as presenting a high risk of future violence will almost certainly be denied parole (Petersilia, 2003, p.190) and will retain a higher security rating than one who is not. Thus, overly-cautious risk-assessments result in longer sentences, higher levels of deprivation, and inevitably, burgeoning prison populations. If the assessment is false, the second guiding principle of the *Parole Act 2002* (s.7(2)(a) "that offenders must not be detained any longer than is consistent with the safety of the community", is frustrated. From the point of view of the criminalized, being held for longer in unnecessarily harsh conditions may engender a loss of faith, and a negative attitude toward the classification system, the parole system, and vicariously toward the society which produces them. Anti-social attitudes may thus be reinforced.

The first author of this article, who has so far served 12 years of a life sentence, has witnessed a number of instances where long-term prisoners, in spite of excellent conduct reports, successful completion of required criminogenic programs, and positive recommendations from unit managers, have been denied parole because of high risk-of-violence assessments. The psychological impact of being denied freedom on the basis of criteria that are opaque, and which may seem unjust, is significant. The men become despondent and cynical, and lose their motivation to prepare for release. Confidence in the competency of psychologists, and trust in the advice of prison managers, is undermined. A growing disdain for 'the system' begins to appear, affecting not only the individual's attitude toward his confinement and his custodians, but also toward the society it represents. Successful post-release adjustment is thereby impaired (Shipley and Arrigo, 2012, p. 40; Szmukler and Rose 2013, p. 134), decreasing the chances of positive future recommendations. The original high risk assessment thus becomes a self-fulfilling prophesy.

Another unfortunate outcome of this anti-rehabilitation, anti-system culture, which often follows an inaccurate risk assessment is that, as noted by Petersilia (2003, p.73), some prisoners will decline even to appear at their parole board hearings, through disillusionment with the process. The outcome for these prisoners is discharge at the very ends of their sentences, with little support from post-release probation authorities. Given that post-parole support and supervision is crucial to community safety, Petersilia (2003, pp.74-75) considers that "the joke is on us". If prisoners disengage with support agencies by boycotting parole, community safety is jeopardized. In this case, the first guiding principle of the *Parole Act 2002* (s.7(1) – "the paramount consideration …[is] the safety of the community" – is undermined. The importance of risk assessments that are transparent, fair and accurate is critical.

THE PROBLEM OF
CROSS-CULTURAL APPLICABILITY

In the international literature, the problem of applying uniform standards cross-culturally is well recognized. This difficulty applies not only to risk-assessment, but also to related areas such as security classification and parole determination. Martel and colleagues (2011), for example, argue that in Canada markers such as substance abuse, community origins, lack of healthy role models, a background of sexual and psychological abuse and low educational levels are high in Canadian Aboriginal communities and automatically mark such persons intrinsically as high risk. Culture-specific risk factors such as a lack of Aboriginal spiritual values and cultural identity are missing from traditional assessment criteria. Moreover, as Andersen (1999) points out, determining precisely what 'traditional' cultural practices and processes were employed, and in which groups, is far from clear. There was in fact huge cultural variety between different tribal groups in pre-colonial Canada. How to accommodate them fairly and accurately in correctional practice is unclear. Moreover, it is not only Indigenous value systems that are at stake. In a field study of Canadian parole hearings, Silverstein (2005) examines some of the practical and ethical problems facing parole boards as they try to grapple with and accommodate multicultural differences – in this case the variation between Aboriginal, Hispanic and Asian prisoners' responsibilization in parole hearings.

In Australia, similar problems are found. Shepherd (2014) and Jones and colleagues (2002), for example, argue for culturally relevant strategies in relation to Indigenous violence prevention programs. Some of the strategies employed in Australia are considered by the authors above, as well as Barclay and Scott (2013). Australia's situation is compared and contrasted with New Zealand's in Newbold and Jeffries (2010).

In a multi-cultural country like New Zealand, where approximately a third of the population is non-European (primarily Maori, Asian and Pacific peoples), cultural factors are an important consideration for the risk assessment process. The largest non-European group is the native New Zealanders, the Maori, which comprise about 15 percent of the total population. As the nation's original inhabitants, Maori have special status in New Zealand, which is recognized in law. Constituting a large social underclass, Maori are also hugely overrepresented in New Zealand's crime statistics (see Newbold, 2000; Newbold and Jeffries, 2010), and constitute around 50 percent of the prison population.

Durie (cited in Coombes and Te Hiwi, 2007, p. 386) notes that Maori often have to "liv[e] with the bad results of the cultural presumptions of Western professionals". This is a well-recognized problem in New Zealand and the Department of Corrections has taken extensive steps to provide for Maori prisoners' needs. It also recognizes that programs based on white European models may be inappropriate for Maori and it has endeavored to create systems that respond to Indigenous ethnic differences. Special needs-assessment procedures have been developed for Maori, and there is a strategy aimed specifically at reducing Maori reoffending. Maori cultural advisers are employed at all major prisons and use of Maori language is encouraged in the workplace. In addition, the Department of Corrections operates dedicated Maori Focus Units within five of its 19 prisons. In comparison with Australia and Canada, however, where Aboriginal populations were culturally diverse with numerous mutually unintelligible languages, traditional Maori culture was relatively uniform and linguistic differences between the regions were not great. So in New Zealand, the problem of indigenization of assessments is simplified.

Notwithstanding this, risk assessment as it currently operates is out of alignment with the cultural difference and Maori perspectives used elsewhere in the corrections system. This makes it difficult to accurately assess Maori risks of future violence. A primary reason is that although specific Maori criminogenic needs are recognized and catered for, the actuarial instruments used in risk assessment are not normed on populations that are culturally representative of Maori (Coombes and Te Hiwi, 2007, p.386). Instead, they are usually normed on white, middle-class populations, amongst which issues like lifestyle violence and alcoholism are far less prominent. When Maori are found to score highly on standardized risk factors, they are therefore deemed to be high risk. Little consideration is given to the fact that certain risk factors tend to be high in many minority groups, largely due to the effects of marginalization, low socio-economic status and high levels of childhood abuse and neglect. They do not necessarily indicate an individual propensity to violence. An additional problem is that in many cases, actuarial instruments are based on unalterable static factors (ibid, p. 383), leaving an individual with a stigmatizing label they are unable to change. Since many of these static factors are found in Maori risk assessments, Maori find themselves burdened with higher security rankings and longer prison time based on criteria that by their nature, cannot change. In spite of the New Zealand Psychological Society's stated ethical obligation to embrace diversity and promote community well-being (Coombes and Te Hiwi, 2007), a form of double marginalization takes place.

THE IMPACT OF PROFESSIONALS

We have contended that risk assessment produces a number of unjust outcomes for those subjected to it, but what of the professionals who do those assessments? There is a body of literature that argues that they too are affected as are the organizations they work for. Arrigo (2013, p. 11), for example, says that "forces of captivity" entrap all who have a stake in the risk assessment process. In regard to psychologists, those forces may be seen within the culture of accountability that pervades the process. For example, Langan (2010, p. 93) notes that risk assessment professionals are expected to minimize public fears by identifying the potentially violent. Those professionals are held accountable by politicians, who are held to account by an ever-fearful public (Szmukler and Rose, 2013, p. 134). In 2003, for example, New Zealand psychiatrist Dr. Peter Fisher was fined $86,000, suspended for six months, and ordered to undergo retraining, for releasing a dangerous mental health patient from custody who stabbed his mother to death the next day. Whether assessment is subjective or actuarial, no process can be 100 percent accurate.

Cases like this, and that of Christie Marceau mentioned above, create a heavy burden for judges and health professionals. The objective inflexibility of risk assessment forces some to assign high risk categories to the criminalized who they do not believe present a real risk, while others may choose to ignore objective indicators and act upon their own judgement. In Dr Fisher's case, this had tragic consequences. The poor predictive power of risk assessment can lead to other negative outcomes for workers. In the United States, the monitoring and regulation of assessment work by a risk-averse employer has been found to contribute to both defensive practice (Langan, 2010, p. 93) and to deliberate, though subtle, deception by employees (Szmukler and Rose, 2013, p. 135). The impact of this "risk colonization" (ibid, p. 134) of the work environment raises many concerns for the psychological profession, both in terms of ethics and in terms of the ability of psychologists to make unbiased assessments when functioning under intense external and internal pressures. Health care professionals must balance the requirement of public safety against the fundamental ethical principle of not causing harm to a client through an inaccurate risk assessment. Balancing client interests against public interests forces the professional to practice within a complex and constrained psycho-legal environment (Shipley and Arrigo, 2012). Arrigo (2013, p. 3) suggests that until risk assessment moves to an approach that does not marginalize people, there will be no overcoming the forces that hold the government, the public, the professionals, the criminalized, and thus society, captive. It is our opinion that, until those forces are overcome, psychologists and violence risk assessors will continue to be subjected to the stress that accompanies being held responsible for the community's safety.

A primary reason for risk assessment being counter-productive to just outcomes concerns the driving force behind it. Risk assessment is largely a response to public fears about the extreme, but rare, instances of violent reoffending that sometimes occur. In New Zealand, a number of highly publicized cases where persons convicted of violent offenses killed whilst on parole, sensitized the public to the danger of releasing violent men without proper monitoring. Examples include Taffy Hotene, who raped and murdered a young woman in 2000; William Bell, who murdered three pensioners in 2001; and Graeme Burton, who killed one person and wounded four others while on parole for murder in 2007. Incidents such as these gave rise to what Szmukler and Rose (2013, p. 126) term a "moral outrage", in which people demanded to know how the incidents happened and, more importantly, how they could have been prevented. Violence risk assessment has been one of the government's main responses to that outrage. It has become a major component of parole board deliberations concerning the interests of public safety (Szmukler and Rose, 2013, pp. 126-127).

Thus, arguably, we can say that the primary focus of risk assessment is not prisoner welfare, but the protection of the community. The assessment process allows correctional and parole authorities to demonstrate an awareness of accredited scientific risk-management practices, while at the same time reducing the concern that accompanies the release of high profile prisoners. Risk assessment is used as much as a practical tool for parole determination and release conditions, as it is a means of assuaging public timorousness (Szmuckler and Rose, 2013, p. 131).

CONCLUSION

We have seen that coincidental with rises in levels of incarceration for those convicted of violent offenses, the use of clinical assessments of risk gave way to actuarial measures in the 1990s. Actuarial measures have the advantage of removing subjectivity and guesswork from the risk assessment process, but they have the disadvantage of being inflexible and not responsive to subtle differences or changes in the circumstances of the criminalized. In recent years, an emphasis on community safety over client welfare has led to a more conservative approach being taken in relation to assessments which disadvantages a large number of persons in conflict with the law. The extra protection that this approach offers the community is minor. Actuarial methods are relatively crude, and struggle to account for ethnic or other individual differences, or to detect subtle changes in an individual's behaviour or outlook. A consequence of this is larger numbers of prisoners being held in high security for longer than is realistically warranted. Such a situation breeds cynicism within prisoners and staff alike. Negative attitudes and low confidence in the efficacy of classification and prison parole systems adversely impact on a person's chances of successful post-release adjustment.

ENDNOTES

* The authors gratefully acknowledge the assistance of Jayne Waugh, Education Officer at Auckland Prison, in the preparation of this article.

REFERENCES

Andersen, Chris (1999) "Governing Aboriginal Justice in Canada: Constructing Responsible Individuals and Communities through 'Tradition'", *Crime, Law & Social Change*, 31: 303-326.

Arrigo, Bruce (2013) "Managing Risk and Marginalizing Identities: On the Society-of-Captives Thesis and the Harm of Social Dis-ease", *International Journal of Offender Therapy & Comparative Criminology*, 57(6): 1-22.

Barclay, Elaine and John Scott (2013) "Australia", in M.K. Nalla and G.R. Newman (eds.), *Community Policing in Indigenous Communities*, London: CRC Press, pp. 153-162.

Brady, Kevin (2009) *Department of Corrections: Managing Offenders On Parole*. Retrieved from: <http://www.oag.govt.nz/2009/parole/part 2.htm>.

Coombes, Leigh, and Erika Te Hiwi (2007) "Social Justice, Community Change", in I.M. Evans, J.J. Rucklidge and M. O'Driscol (eds.), *Professional Practice of Psychology in Aotearoa New Zealand*, Wellington: New Zealand Psychological Society. pp. 379-396.

Jones, Robin, Mary Masters, Alison Griffiths and Nicole Moulday (2002) "Culturally Relevant Assessment of Indigenous Offenders: A Literature Review", *Australian Psychologist*, 37(3): 187-197.

Langan, Joan (2010) "Challenging Assumptions About Risk Factors and the Role of Screeningfor Violence Risk in the Field of Mental Health", *Health, Risk & Society*, 12(2): 85-100.

Large, Matthew and Olav Nielssen (2011) "Probability and Loss: Two Sides of the Risk Assessment Coin", *The Psychiatrist*, 35(11): 413-418.

Martel, Joane, Renée Brassard and Mylène Jaccoud (2011) "When Two Worlds Collide: Aboriginal Risk Management in Canadian Corrections", *British Journal of Criminology*, 51(2): 235-255.

Newbold, Greg (2007) *The Problem of Prisons: Corrections Reform in New Zealand Since 1840*, Wellington: Dunmore Publishing.

Newbold, Greg (2002) *Crime in New Zealand,* Palmerston North: Dunmore Press.

Newbold, Greg and Samantha Jeffries (2010) "Race, Crime and Criminal Justice in Australia and New Zealand", in A. Kalunta-Crumpton (ed.), *Race, Crime and Criminal Justice: International Perspectives*, Hampshire: Palgrave Macmillan, pp. 187-206.

Opie, Anne (2012) *Outlaw to Citizen: Making the Transition from Prison in New Zealand*, Auckland: Dunmore Publishing Ltd.

Petersilia, Joan (2003) *When Prisoners Come Home: Parole and Prisoner Reentry,* New York: Oxford University Press.

Shepherd, Stephanie (2014) "Finding Color in Conformity: A Commentary on Culturally Specific Risk Factors for Violence in Australia", *International Journal of Offender Therapy and Comparative Criminology,* June: 1-11.

Silverstein, Martin (2005) ""What's Race Got to Do with Justice?" Resposibilization Strategies at Parole Hearings", *British Journal of Criminology,* 45: 340-454.

Spier, Philip (2002) *Reconviction and Reimprisonment Rates for Released Prisoners,* Wellington: Ministry of Justice.

Shipley, Stacey and Bruce Arrigo (2012) *Introduction to Forensic Psychology: Court, Law Enforcement, and Correctional Practices* (third edition), San Diego: Elsevier Academic Press.

Szmukler, George and Nicholas Rose (2013) "Risk Assessment in Mental Health Care: Values and Costs", *Behavioral Sciences and the Law,* 31(1): 125-140.

ABOUT THE AUTHORS

Daniel Luff is serving a life sentence at Auckland Prison, New Zealand, for killing a policeman and wounding another in 2002. Daniel Luff was 17 years old at the time. Since then he has graduated with a BA in psychology from Massey University, New Zealand, and in 2014 won the university's "Outstanding Achiever's Award" for obtaining an 'A' grade average over a 24-month period. He is currently studying for his MA by distance education.

Greg Newbold is Professor in Sociology at the University of Canterbury, New Zealand. In the late 1970s he served a seven and a half year sentence for selling heroin and achieved his MA while in maximum security at Auckland Prison. He studied for his PhD after his release. Greg Newbold has written seven books and over 80 scholarly articles, and is currently one of New Zealand's leading criminologists.

Seeing Shame:
Legal Storytelling and Prisoner Rehabilitation
Alan Mobley

"It was the best of times, it was the worst of times".

– Charles Dickens (1859)

INTRODUCTION

In this unprecedented era of mass incarceration, prison reform and prisoner reentry have taken on great salience. Many jurisdictions are reformulating policy to keep people out of prisons and under correctional control in their home communities (Pew Center on the States, 2009; Mobley, 2011; Sentencing Project, 2014). The public safety implications of this move are a major concern. The compromise that seems to be taking shape is one in which an expanded "treatment" or "rehabilitative" side of corrections arises to bolster the more punitive and enduring incapacitation side. Both sides would share the goal of supporting "offenders" in desistance from crime.

Many scholars of the desistance process point to the important role played by formerly incarcerated persons acting as prisoner mentors and rehabilitation program staff (Maruna, 2001; Maruna and LeBel, 2009; Harris, 2011; Calverley, 2012). Ex-cons, ex-gang members and ex-addicts appear as highly valued partners in this emergent correctional scheme. With such large numbers of "ex's" moving from custodial environments to mainstream society, we might stop a moment to reflect on why proportionally so few step forward as mentors. In this paper, I will share my thoughts, or rather, my thoughts and feelings on this important topic. I offer up my emotions, in particular the emotion of shame, because I believe that shame stemming from my own incarceration experience has motivated my self-exclusion from much prison-related work, including work as a prison volunteer mentor.

What follows revolves around a first person account of my experience of trying to become a prison volunteer. The narrative is informed by "legal storytelling", for which I offer a brief introduction. I use the legal storytelling method because it allows me to discuss an emotionally challenging topic in a manner that is somewhat detached and, thus, less personally painful. My storytelling is also informed by the practice of "Council" (Zimmerman and Coyle, 1996). Like legal storytelling, Council supports the practice of sharing with peers deeply meaningful and challenging thoughts and feelings. Council, however, also promotes "speaking from the heart", a practice that is perhaps the opposite of "detached". According to Center for Council (2014, p. 4):

> Council is a modern practice derived from many ancient forms of communicating in a circle. Sometimes referred to as "Listening Circles", Council utilizes a center, a circle and a talking piece to create an intentional space in which to share our stories. The practice of deep listening without judgment fosters an atmosphere of respect for ourselves and for others, and promotes empathy, dissolving barriers to cooperation, understanding and community.

Both methods of communication have proven useful to me in identifying personal obstacles impeding my very public work in prison communities. I continue to have a deep desire to serve prisoners and their communities. Part of the rationale for this paper is my growing awareness that if I am to provide effective service I must do so in a satisfying and sustainable way. The principal means by which I currently work with prisoners is as a researcher and in supporting direct services, particularly Council. My hope is to build upon and expand this work, and facilitate the complementary work of others. To do so will require navigating many hurdles, one of which is the challenge of managing strong emotions.

In the preparation of this paper, and in prison work more generally, I am inspired by the hopeful words of a leading scholar on restorative justice and shame who notes: "shame is a sign of a severed or threatened social bond, but communication about shame can bring people closer together and heal that bond" (Van Stokkom, 2002, p. 343). This then, is a hopeful move toward contributing to justice reform and healing.

PRISON SCHOLARSHIP AND ME

Recent contributions to the scholarly study of prisons have left this student of the genre overwhelmed. My problem lies both with the quality and quantity. Let me explain. My work involves action research on imprisonment and the criminal justice system. When I began this avenue of inquiry the year was 1990 and I resided in a prison cell. The number of books and articles available for research was severely limited by my circumstances, to be sure, but what I did find was prison sociology dating from the 1950s-1970s. As a prisoner who thought he "knew it all" about prison, I was surprised by what I found. The work I encountered portrayed prisoners as complex human beings and prisons as deeply troubled institutions. This felt real and was gratifying for me. When I was granted my freedom a few years later, I continued to find prison studies enlightening and as a doctoral student an emotionally compelling literature was critical to my goals.

Times, however, have changed. I dare say that today's vast scholarly production on imprisonment far surpasses in quantity what was produced in the 1950s through to the 1970s. As for quality, the work continues to be very smart and very informative in its way, but at times I find something missing. I suspect that my unease relates to a lack of dignity and humanity accorded to participants in the legal process. I do not feel this same void, however, when I read stories and first-person accounts of incarceration (see especially the *Journal of Prisoners on Prisons*), whether from the perspective of the prison guard (e.g. Conover, 2010), the prisoner (e.g. Hassine and Wright, 1996; Baca, 2007), the parolee (e.g. Gonnerman, 2005), the prison educator (e.g. Matlin, 2005), or the children of incarcerated parents (e.g. Bernstein, 2007). Offering a first-person narrative of my experience of trying to become a prison volunteer is meant as a contribution to a penological literature that has grown vast and heady, but may have lost its heart. My aim is not to criticize or supplant other offerings. What I hope to do is complement the existing literature by providing a narrative with a certain *sensibility* – namely, the complexity of lived experience. In this way, perhaps each scholarly orientation may work to enrich the other.

BECOMING A CONVICT CRIMINOLOGIST

Convict criminology embraces narratives of lived experience (Ross and Richards, 2003). At the time of convict criminology's founding in the mid-1990s, however, I had to admit that I was a reluctant co-founder. As a graduate student I had detected feelings of shame in my nascent professional identity. As a fledgling state-employed teaching assistant/criminologist I saw myself complicit in the burgeoning prison-industrial complex. In my academic department, colleagues were happy about the expansion of resources and rapid growth in the numbers of faculty and students. On the other side of town, at my fieldwork sites in South-Central and East Los Angeles, the people who resided there were also aware of the length and breadth of the prison-industrial complex. The difference was, they called its operation "genocide".

I told myself that my role was okay because I could make a positive difference. Others said so as well, but still I doubted it was true. I had lived in the belly of the beast for ten years, and was now living within the constricted world of parole. I had seen the drug war up close and personal, watched the proliferation of new laws and their craftily worded rationales, and noted that many occupational groups were getting fat off of crime (Gilmore, 2007). Even me. In the parlance of the street, I was "getting paid". I had a fellowship at a major research university, was beginning a career in an expanding, reputable field and was receiving some minor accolades. None of this was going to end any time soon. But was this right? Was I living an honourable life? My fieldwork with action research participants—friends and colleagues—brought the troubling realization that I did not know for sure.

Now, years later, as a more fully credentialed convict criminologist, I continue to wonder. Having as the anthropologists say, "gone native" long ago, I make no pretense to scientific objectivity, and I find few barriers between my work and the rest of my life. And although I hope this approach enriches my work, I should point out it often creates a mess. What I mean is that certain aspects of my scholarly research and life experience strike me (and others) as synergistic. These life spheres, important and provocative on their own, when connected produce additional insights. My trouble is that I find great difficulty tying them neatly together. I often encounter a block and I suspect that at its source, or at least part of this block, is shame.

WHY FEEL SHAME?

> When shamed, people feel physically, psychologically, and socially diminished. There is a dramatic shift in one's perception and experience of the self. People in the midst of a shame experience feel small, inferior, unworthy, or even despicable (Tangney *et al.*, 2011a, p. 711).

Shame is commonly thought of as being, well, shameful. Researchers tell us that in general, people of all types tend to avoid discussions of shame (Retzinger and Scheff, 2000; Tangney *et al.*, 2011b). If this is true of most people, it is probably even more so for prisoners and former prisoners who bear the burden of criminal records and the attending social stigma.

Within criminology, the importance of shame is becoming more readily acknowledged. Braithwaite's (1989) theory of reintegrative shaming is probably most responsible for this. Braithwaite argues that the criminal legal process is rife with shaming. Braithwaite's point is that the justice process is disintegrative, in that it further separates "offenders" from law-abiding "communities". Reintegrative shaming condemns the unlawful act, but in contrast to conventional shaming, makes certain to affirm the personhood of the bad actor. The affirmation process is accomplished by showing respect to the wrongdoer and, importantly, making sure s/he has a way of regaining good standing in the community. Adding to this problematic is a recent study of the theory of reintegrative shaming by Botchkovar and Tittle (2005, p. 432), who note that "our results suggest that shaming of any kind, whether reintegrative or disintegrative, may have pejorative consequences".

When I ask myself why I seldom go back into prisons, the usual justifications arise: prisons are remote; getting in is a hassle; staff are often difficult. Less appealing explanations concern the shame sensations I feel when I am there. Why do I feel what I feel? Have I not regained good standing in the community? Shame researcher June Tangney and colleagues (2011a, p. 711), looking into shame in criminal justice processes, cite a typical response to shame: "The knee-jerk response is not to apologize and repair but rather to hide or escape. This is understandable because the pain is great, the self is impaired, and the job (to transform the self from fundamentally flawed to good) is impossibly immense".

In *The New Jim Crow*, author Michelle Alexander (2010, p. 162) quotes Dorcey Nunn, a former prisoner and long-time advocate for the restoration of full human rights to felons. Nunn points out that shame is a major part of the lived experience of currently and formerly incarcerated people:

The biggest hurdle you gotta get over when you walk out those prison gates is shame—that shame, that stigma, that label, that thing you wear around your neck saying 'I'm a criminal'. It's like a yoke around your neck, and it'll drag you down, and even kill you if you let it.

What sociologist Harold Garfinkle (1956) famously has called, "status degradation ceremonies" are integral to the justice process. In prisons, degradation and humiliation are especially well represented. To give you a vicarious experience of this I offer a descriptive analogy of prison that I have used before (Mobley, 2010, p. 15), and that has resonated strongly with prisoners:

The analogy that presents itself as most like the psychological cesspool of prison is the locker room: a high school or college locker room for male athletes.

In your mind's eye fill out the room, if you will, with damp and sweat, stench, and soiled belongings. Now put in place a large number – too large for the room – of opposing athletes. Watch some gamely strut and posture while others withdraw into self-imposed isolation, daydreams, and consuming, reflexive thought. Feel the hyper masculinity manifest in shouted expletives and grunting sexual innuendo. Observe the sophomoric humor and carelessly displayed bodily functions. Think of those participating in the antics as World Wrestling performers. See their legendary menace and outrageous, provocative acts.

Next, consider quite seriously that they are not acting, that they see their individual performances as competitive and vital to their identity, integrity and personal safety. Consider that they view one another as lethal threats.

Now, throw into the locker room one or two officials who are paid to keep an eye on things, but who make their top priority going home safely every night. Finally, go ahead and step into the locker room yourself and seal the door behind you. How do you feel? If you have conscientiously engaged in this exercise you now have a reasonable approximation of prison. If you have been unable to concentrate fully, go ahead and try it again, and again, and again. There is plenty of time for trial and error, to vary your inflection, to get it right. The exercise, like the page upon which it is written, is not going anywhere, and, as a convict, neither are you.

Enjoy your stay.

I submit that prisons stink with shame. Shame is finding yourself stuck in the cesspool with little if anything you can do about it. You are an object being acted upon, and not kindly. For the (ex-)convict part of me, reliving those shaming experiences is tough. For the criminologist part of me, going into prisons and bearing witness to others' shame, maybe even being a catalyst for it, troubles me as well.

PRISON VOLUNTEER ORIENTATION:
MY STORY OF TRAUMA AND SELF-EXCLUSION

I have been serving on the advisory board of a prison meditation program for some five years. Recently I decided to apply to go into the prison as a volunteer. Being a formerly incarcerated person, I wondered if I would be allowed to do so. The application process entails completing a form revealing one's vital statistics, current life and work details, and past criminal record. The process includes attending a mandatory day-long orientation for new volunteers, who, should they wish to continue as repeat volunteers, are then required to attend the orientation annually.

I wanted to go into prison and sit with prisoners as a way of giving back to a community from which I have learned so much. I also sought this opportunity as a tangible way of moving forward in my life, and, in a sense, putting the trauma of the prison experience behind me. I felt I was ready for this. After all, fifteen years had passed since I had done my time. And although I felt nervous about the prospect of re-entering prison to instruct or even just sit with prisoners, I thought myself able to handle the anxiety. I practice yoga and meditation nearly every day, lead and participate in talking circles centered on the justice process and healing, and am established in my post-prison career as a criminologist and professor. What could go wrong?

There were four of us from the prison meditation program scheduled to attend the orientation this particular Saturday. Two of us were going for our first time and two were repeat volunteers. The season was early spring in southern California, meaning there were low clouds, rain and general gloom. At 7:30am I was ready to go but I did not want to be the one to drive. I rarely drive and have never enjoyed driving as it often makes me nervous. However, now that I have a large sedan, a Crown Victoria, I feel the need to offer. Before I have a chance to offer to drive, one of the other volunteers asks me if I might. He does it in a way that makes it easy for me to back out, but the fact that he brought it up indicates what he thinks makes the most sense. So I drive. Not because I want to or because it does not matter to me, but because a reasonable person expects that the person with the Crown Vic should drive. It is raining moderately hard when I pull-out of the driveway and cross the double yellow lines heading south. The weighty boys in the back seat bring the rear of the car down to kiss the road and off we go. The drive passes without notable incident. Our banter rises and falls and feels fairly easy. Traffic is very light. There comes a moment when I say something and someone asks for clarification and I sort of bite back. I use the word "motherfucker" to convey my point. I hear myself, and sort of wonder where that comment came from. I wonder if they wonder too.

We arrive at the prison and I decide not to bring a pen. While I should probably muse aloud about the issue, in which case I am sure someone would say, "oh, yeah bring pens", I keep my thoughts to myself because I am uptight. Just seeing the enormity of the place: the administration building, the gun towers, and the "secure housing unit" makes my asshole pucker. There are two rows of twelve foot, chain-link, and razor wire-topped fence with the customary ten feet of gravel in between. The gun towers sit right above that strip of no man's land. Any prisoner skillful enough to get past the first fence—the electrified one – yet unfortunate enough to find themselves found in the middle, would soon attest to the fabled moniker of that place: the kill zone.

It is still raining so I pull the hood of my jacket down over my face, lower my head and walk. I nearly say aloud what I am thinking: that at least the rain has forced me to keep my head down and not look around. The short walk to the buildings feels like skirting a rocky outcropping way up high, where the guide admonishes, "don't look down", because she does not want you to be spooked by seeing the prospect of certain death below. Inversely, I was looking down because I was nervous about looking up. If I were to look up I would take note of the always startling fact that, from the outside, prisons are ghost towns. They are eerily quiet and almost nothing moves. This perception of nothingness mirrors the feeling of being in prison, where I at least often felt myself a nonentity, held in stasis while the world passed me by.

Going into the administration building I see framed portraits of the usual suspects: the state Governor, the Secretary of Corrections and the Warden. Smiling jackals all. Their power ties and business suits contrast sharply with the dull walls, institutional flooring and florescent lights. The hallway is wide and the first corner brings the sounds of perhaps two-dozen would be volunteers waiting for the conference room to open.

They are black, brown and white, nearly all male, with the lone female looking to me soft, vulnerable, and more than slightly out of place. It seems to me that she thinks she will be all right in an almost all male environment. Right. I recognize one of the African American men as a pastor – he wears a high, starched white collar and a broad brimmed black hat and smiles like he is at a wedding. Ironically, to me he looks as though he is ready to preside over a funeral. I also recognize a Latino man that I believe to be named Velez or Valdez. I cannot quite place where I know him from, but I see him wearing a blue suit and as having a high-level bureaucrat's aggressive attitude. I fail to acknowledge either of them and neither offers any recognition of me.

A tall man, thin but rounded in the middle, balding, glasses, smiling lips under unsmiling eyes, comes around the corner carrying an umbrella high over his head. His jovial manner tells me that he works here so he must be the chaplain. His frivolity could be explained by the fact that he is getting paid to be here, and that he does not care at all about being late. He opens the doors and we file in. At first glance, it is clear that there are not enough chairs around the conference tables to accommodate all of us. I decide that sitting in the cheap folding chairs along the wall will be okay with me. I follow the man in front of me the long way around the tables and, sure enough, we wind up along the wall, near to the front. Being in a good position to have their volunteer documents checked, perhaps those sitting toward the front are likely to leave first.

I look around the room in a way that I often do at parties, to see what I can see by way of refuge – crowded rooms make me uncomfortable, so I am always looking for a safe haven, a niche and a congenial person to talk to. Often, I choose to speak to an older person or someone who strikes me as likely to remain on the periphery of things. Sometimes I choose the most beautiful woman in the room, although I do so rarely anymore. The interesting thing is that my eyes find no hold. There is not a single face I feel drawn to in any way. No one strikes me as offering respite from this place and its purpose. When I mentally rejoin the others and turn toward the front to pay attention to what the chaplain is about to say, I resign myself to the allies I have come with, on my left and right, and none other.

"This is a prison!", so begins the chaplain.

"This is a prison!"

He seems to make it his mission to demonize the place and its denizens as fully as possible. He speaks of shanks and other weapons, of sexual assault, coercion, cooptation, and riots. He assures us that if we are taken captive the State will not bargain for our release. He says it all with an understated smile.

I find myself utterly 'freaked out'. Being within these walls and in proximity to prisoners and prison authorities has me in fight or flight mode. I look to Pete to see how he is handling it. He notices my distress and whispers that he is doing a "soft belly" breath meditation. I say, "yeah, I know what you're talking about", and I think I do, but I do not do anything about it. Whatever I am holding is not so much in my belly. I am tired and getting hungry and the chaplain will not let up with his, "This is a prison!" business.

"This is a place of evil. You will be safe, but the prisoners are not. This is a dark, violent, and dangerous place".

Yeah, I get it. I remember. All the stories and details he lays out help me to remember. And then his summation brings it all home, catching me vulnerable, in that chair for over three hours. He says that "inmates" lead half-lives, maybe less than that. "Inmates" are deprived, and needy. When they see free people they often cannot help themselves. They soak up or otherwise suck in all the freedom they can. We volunteers should not take it personally. The "inmates" are not after us as individuals, but as a means to an end. The end goal, something they may not even be aware of, is filling the void and lessening deprivation. We need to watch out for them.

At that moment, I realize I am ashamed. And then I feel ashamed of feeling ashamed. My initial shame comes from having been an "inmate" and from having lived such a pathetic, reduced existence. I remember times when I went to the chapel to meet with volunteers. It is true that I sensed in them something that I found lacking in myself. I felt shy and somewhat of a lesser person around them because of that sensation. I hungered for their attention and to hear anything they had to say. Sometimes the excitement would be so great that I would feel "down" after they left. That "down time" was hard time and if I did not watch myself, it became precarious time. In other words, when a prisoner is feeling down he tends to pay less attention to his surroundings. And in a place where people take offense at clumsiness and lack of consideration (respect), being absentminded or resentful of one's predicament can lead to trouble.

Now I was preparing to put myself in the role of volunteer, of outsider, of possessor of that which prisoners could never, ever, have, yet so hungered for. Was I really willing to become a trigger for the rollercoaster ride of desperate men? Do not get me wrong: I very much appreciated the folks who came in to teach, preach to and mentor us. Still do. But at the same time, I cannot deny the pain brought on by their presence. Easy time means keeping your mind and body in the same place, which may be summed up with the phrase: be here now. Do the time and do not let the time do you. Mixing with free people threatens that mantra. It puts your head in the streets. I avoided free people for many years, and only made my way to the chapel when I had tired of that way of thinking and acting and had "broken weak" or succumbed to the urge to seek help. Yes, I gained from these experiences, no doubt. However, there is a part of me that still would not wish that bumpy ride on anybody.

Following this experience, the orientation, I have not gone back to volunteer in the prison, although the prison did call to say I was approved to go inside for the next year. I was somewhat surprised, but did not act on the information. Some of the other volunteers asked me about it a few times, but I put them off until they stopped asking. How did this happen? How did my plan to help others locked inside and in so doing help myself become circumvented? I do not have definitive answers. What I do have to offer is this story and a fledgling analysis that hinges on shame. Not only could I not face the prison, the staff, or the prisoners without a great deal of anxiety and worry, most of all I could not face myself. Not the me I had once been, nor the me I hope I am now.

LEGAL STORYTELLING: A USEFUL WORKAROUND?

> Shamed people feel the eyes of others on them, even when experiencing the emotion in solitude. (Tangney *et al.*, 2011a, p. 711).

I have offered a personal story that I think carries the ambiguity and messiness of a real first-person account. The story involved my struggles with volunteering for a local prison program. I put forward this story in the hope that it might provide insights into the specifics of formerly incarcerated persons' reluctance to go back inside and more generally to describe some of the many difficulties in post-release living.

My storytelling can perhaps be best seen as falling within the tradition of legal storytelling pioneered by Bell (1992) and Delgado (2009). Richard Delgado describes legal storytelling as important, even crucial to our understanding of law and legal processes. Storytelling is important as it allows the narrator to take an unpopular position. Rather than represent itself as objective, neutral and outside or above the realm of human experience, legal storytelling embraces the human aspect of materiality. It is scholarship that positions itself not as transcendent or pertaining to the "law in books", but work that expresses something of the lived reality of law, which may be more accurately described as the "law in action" (Calavita, 2010). And it does so from the marginalized point of view of dispossessed out-group members. Further, Delgado (2007) argues that legal storytelling is useful both to groups that "get it" and can relate to the stories of the oppressed, as well as to their opponents, the "in group" members who are challenged to understand. Delgado writes:

> Legal storytelling is an engine built to hurl rocks over walls of social
> complacency that obscure the view out from the citadel. But the rocks all
> have messages tied to them that the defenders cannot help but read. The
> messages say, let us knock down the walls, and use the blocks to pave a
> road we can all walk together (ibid, p. 20).

The formerly incarcerated are charter members of the oppressed. A generation of discriminatory law making, set out in painful detail in *The New Jim Crow* (Alexander, 2010), has deepened the material and symbolic implications of their felon status. They have found their actions criminalized, even when the same behaviours when committed by non-felons are not. In this vein of socially constructed reality, "criminality" in the form of street crime has become increasingly concentrated in fewer places and among fewer people. If conventional wisdom is correct, this administrative and statistical reality may well lead to former felons becoming increasingly feared, and the chances of their rehabilitation more heavily disparaged. Without significant success, new more progressive policies like those supportive of re-entry may give way to a resurgence of punitive justice strategies.

FRAMING THE STORY:
CAUTIONARY TALES

Two lines of research come together here. The first comes to us from Rosenfeld and colleagues (2005) who suggests that high felon recidivism rates and falling overall crime rates mean that ex-prisoners are responsible for an increasing proportion of crime. Rosenfeld's quantitative analysis indicates that while most citizens are crime-free, the formerly incarcerated remain exceptionally crime-prone. These findings related specifically to certain persons complement research on places with high levels of law enforcement contact. Together they suggest that location matters when examining recidivism – although the overall crime rate may rise and fall, aggregation actually obscures important facts related to place (Clear, 2007). Namely, that while some places are becoming ever "safer", at least in terms of reported crime, other places are not (see Wacquant, 2009; Hedges and Sacco, 2012, on "sacrifice zones"). Perhaps, not coincidentally, the high numbers of formerly incarcerated persons that Rosenfeld suggests are becoming responsible for much crime, live in the very same places that geographic analysis suggests are most worrisome. In sum, while national-level crime rates continue to decline, criminal involvement remains persistently in place where former felons reside – namely, in poorer and disadvantaged neighborhoods.

The second relevant line of research concerns rehabilitation and the possibility of desistance from crime. Advocates of "smart" sentencing and holistic prisoner reentry strategies (Travis, 2005) suggest that we begin attending to the needs of felons as soon as possible. This suggests that the successful reentry and rehabilitation of "offenders" should begin at sentencing, and time in custody needs to be an opportunity for service delivery. The type of personnel that staff felon rehabilitation programs matters. Those with greater empathy and ability to relate to prisoners are better able to elicit more positive program results (Wexler *et al.*, 1999). This finding is especially pronounced in substance abuse treatment settings (Leon, 1995; Welsh and Zajac, 2004). Surveys indicate that up to 80 percent of convicted populations have problems with drug abuse that contribute to their criminality (Inciardi *et al.*, 2004). It is unsurprising, then, that substance abuse programs are among the most common prison rehabilitative programs available.

In bringing these two lines of research together, I mean to highlight the fact that felons can be helped to desist from crime; meaning that recidivism is not a foregone conclusion. Persons convicted of felonies can be assisted to find dignity, purpose and meaning in crime-free, post-prison lives. Such help may best come from people who are empowered by their own life experiences of prison and reentry. Consequently, it seems important that we ask how the formerly incarcerated can be inspired and supported to "give back" by participating in rehabilitation programs. Not only would their involvement improve the lives and life chances of some of the most vulnerable among us, but also, structural factors notwithstanding, gains in prison programs could result in diminished crime in places that appear to be the most risky.

Of course, it is widely known that ex-prisoners are often found staffing substance abuse treatment programs. When asked, they tell us that "giving back" contributes mightily to their own "recovery", both from drugs and crime (Terry, 2003). In sum, they credit their own program participation, whether as client or staff, for keeping them safe and free. Since this is the case, the present endeavour has explored why there are not more ex-prisoner run programs available. If program participation is a key to post-incarceration success, and if working as a program staff member is a niche already open to the formerly incarcerated, then why do so few take up the vocation? Many, if not most, programs directed at "criminals" and addicts can boast ex-prisoners among their staff, but with approximately 700,000 people exiting prisons and another million or so leaving jails each year, why do so few take the opportunity to improve themselves, stay safe, and give back?

The structural impediments to post release life, or the "collateral consequences" of imprisonment, that are so familiar to the formerly incarcerated (Mauer and Chesney-Lind, 2002), are only one aspect of the barriers to giving back. What I emphasize here, through story, is self-exclusion, or the practice of effectively barring oneself from participation in justice-related activities. In focusing on self-exclusion I do not mean to suggest that the personal and subjective are totally distinct from more structural impediments to service. In fact, I think they go hand-in-hand. Although this essay does not detail the many structural impediments to service activities, such as those barring association among known felons, implicit is the suggestion that the presence of formal proscriptions and other civic barriers contribute to self-exclusion.

One of the most obvious and discussed examples of structural or civic barriers concerns employment applications and the infamous "box" asking whether or not applicants have been convicted of a felony. The mere presence of this question on job application forms has discouraged countless former-felon jobseekers from engaging in the application process (Western, 2006; Alexander, 2010). Whether or not their felon status would ultimately exclude them from consideration for employment, the perception that it probably would discourages many from even trying.

Advocates for the formerly incarcerated have launched a campaign to "ban the box" (Alexander, 2010). This initiative is intended to give jobseekers and employers a chance to get to know each other through the job application process *before* the applicant's felon status is revealed. Advocates have high hopes that this reform will influence former felons to give society a chance to accept them, even as they take the necessary steps to integrate themselves into civic culture.

CONCLUSION: PRISON AS AN ENDURING SITE OF SHAME

The personal shame that I have described seems to come from my prison experience, and yet has been compounded by my reentry from prison and into the professional role of a "convict criminologist" (see *Journal of Prisoners on Prisons*, 2012). Accordingly, I have offered some exploratory analysis suggesting why these situations could give rise to shame and how shame might provoke self-exclusion from what is presumed to be a satisfying, appropriate, and even lucrative vocation.

As far as feeling conflicting emotions around justice-related work, I know I am not the only criminologist who has felt this way (Cohen, 1988), nor the only formerly incarcerated activist. Does it make a difference that I am both criminologist and ex-con? Are my feelings of complicity and shame ratcheted up a notch because of my hybrid status? If so, perhaps the relative clarity offered by my social location may provide something of value to my more conventionally situated colleagues, the felons and the scholars and activists who study and serve them.

If are we serious about finding ways to meaningfully reduce felon recidivism, we need to foster the participation of reformed ex-prisoners in prisoner rehabilitation programs. To do so, we may need to actively facilitate and support their healing from the pains of their own imprisonment. Better yet, we ought to think about doing away altogether with the shame that comes with incarceration (Harris and Maruna, 2006). In a similar way, the literature on prisons would benefit from the "symbolic reparation" (Retzinger and Scheff, 2000, p. 8) supplied by voices with direct experience. These two issues, fostering ex-prisoner involvement in prison programming and the current lack of prisoner voices in prison sociology, are both matters of inclusion, and may be related. Since imprisonment is burdened by shame and shame is uncomfortable to witness as well as to experience, we must consider whether the field of penology (un) knowingly marginalizes imprisoned voices because it finds them painful to hear. Of course this is not the whole story and there exist many technical challenges to prison research: distant facilities, cumbersome visitation rules, restrictions barring research and so on. What I mean to emphasize here is the emotional state of the potential researcher or prison volunteer. Yes, impediments "out there" in the structures of prisons in society exist and have consequences, but so too do issues on the "inside".

As Retzinger and Scheff (2000, p. 12) have argued in a discussion of reintegrative shaming in restorative justice conferences, we all need to get more comfortable with shame:

If as Goffman and others have argued, normal shame and embarrassment are an almost continuous part of all human contact, we can see why the visible expression of shame by the offender looms so large in symbolic reparation. When we see signs of shame and embarrassment in others, we are able to recognize them as human beings like ourselves, no matter the language, cultural setting, or context. The central role of shame in human contact has long been recognized in the scientific-humanist tradition, as expressed by Darwin, Neitzsche, Sartre, and many others. To understand the way that successful conferences run on normal reintegrative shame, one needs to overcome the view of shame as a disgraceful emotion, to be denied and hidden from self and other.

I encourage further research on the links between shame and incarceration, recidivism, and the participation of former felons in re-entry and rehabilitation programs. I also call upon the field of penology, and criminology more generally, to examine its reluctance to more actively collaborate with the people who are often made the subjects of research. And finally, to imprisoned and formerly incarcerated potential writers, seek help to cope with shame if you experience it and let your voices be heard.

ENDNOTES

* I offer deep appreciation to the editors and peer reviewers of this journal. Without your help this fledgling attempt at exploring a tough topic would not have seen print. I also thank my colleagues at Center for Council and the monastic community of Deer Park Monastery for their unwavering support of healing, of all sorts.

REFERENCES

Alexander, Michelle (2010) *The New Jim Crow*, New York: New Press.

Bell, Daniel (1992) *Faces at the Bottom of the Well: The Permanence of Racism*, New York: Basic Books.

Baca, Jimmy Santiago (2007) *A Place to Stand,* New York, Grove Press.

Bernstein, Nell (2007) *All Alone in the World*, New York: New Press.

Botchkovar, Ekaterina V. and Charles R. Tittle (2005) "Crime, Shame and Reintegration in Russia", *Theoretical Criminology*, 9(4): 401-442.

Braithwaite, John (1989) *Crime, Shame and Reintegration*, New York: Cambridge University Press.

Calavita, Kitty (2010) *Invitation to Law and Society: An Introduction to the Study of Real Law,* Chicago: University of Chicago Press.

Calverley, Adam (2012) *Cultures of Desistance: Rehabilitation, Reintegration and Ethnic Minorities*, Abingdon: Routledge.

Center for Council (2014) <http://www.centerforcouncil.org/>.

Clear, Todd (2007) *Imprisoning Communities,* Oxford: Oxford University Press.

Cohen, Stanley (1988) *Against Criminology*, New Brunswick (NJ): Transaction.

Conover, Ted. (2010) *Newjack: Guarding Sing Sing*, New York: Vintage.

Delgado, Richard (2009) "Storytelling for Oppositionists and Others", A. K. Wing and J. Stefancic (eds.), *The Law Unbound! A Richard Delgado Reader,* Boulder (CO): Paradigm Publishers.

Dickens, Charles (1859) *A Tale of Two Cities*, London: Chapman & Hall.

Garfinkle, Harold (1956) "The Conditions of Successful Status Degradation Ceremonies", *The American Journal of Sociology,* 5: 420-424.

Gilmore, Ruth W. (2007) *Golden Gulag*, Berkeley (CA): University of California Press.

Gonnerman, Jennifer (2005) *Life on the Outside: The Prison Odyssey of Elaine Bartlett,* New York: Picador.

Harris, Nathan and Shadd Maruna (2006) "Shame, Shaming and Restorative Justice: A Critical Appraisal", in Dennis Sullivan and Larry Tifft (eds.), *Handbook of Restorative Justice: A Global Perspective,* New York: Routledge, pp. 452-460.

Harris, Alexes (2011) "Constructing Clean Dreams: Accounts, Future Selves, and Social and Structural Support as Desistance Work", *Symbolic Interaction,* 34(1): 63-85.

Hassine, Victor and Richard A. Wright (1996) *Life Without Parole: Living in Prison Today*, Thomas J. Bernard and Richard McCleary (eds.), Los Angeles: Roxbury Publishing Company.

Hedges, Chris and Joe Sacco (2012) *Days of Destruction, Days of Revolt,* New York: Nation Books.

Inciardi, James A., Steven S. Martin and Clifford A. Butzin (2004) "Five-year Outcomes of Therapeutic Community Treatment of Drug-involved Offenders After Release from Prison", *Crime & Delinquency,* 50(1): 88-107.

Journal of Prisoners on Prisons (2012) "A Special Issue Commemorating the 15th Anniversary of Convict Criminology", 21(1&2).

Leon, George De (1995) "Therapeutic Communities for Addictions: A Theoretical Framework", *Substance Use & Misuse,* 30(12): 1603-1645.

Maruna Shadd (2001) Making Good: *How Ex-Convicts Reform and Rebuild their Lives,* Washington (DC): American Psychological Association Books.

Maruna, Shadd and Tom LeBel (2009) "Strengths-Based Approaches to Reentry: Extra Mileage toward Reintegration and Destigmatization", *Japanese Journal of Sociological Criminology,* 34: 58-80.

Matlin, David (2005) *Prisons: Inside the New America: From Vernooykill Creek to Abu Ghraib*, Berkeley: North Atlantic Books.

Mauer, Marc and Meda Chesney-Lind (eds.) (2002) *Invisible Punishment*, New York: New Press.

Mobley, Alan (2011) "Decarceration Nation? Penal Downsizing and the Human Security Framework", *Western Criminology Review*, 12(2).

Mobley, Alan (2010) "Garbage In, Garbage Out? The Convict Code and Participatory Prison Reform", in M. Maguire (ed.), *Critical Issues of Crime and Justice: Thought, Policy and Practice,* Los Angeles: Sage.

Pew Center on the States (2009) *One in 31: The Long Reach of American Corrections*, Washington (DC): The Pew Charitable Trusts.

Retzinger, Suzanne M. and Thomas J. Scheff (2000) "Shame and Shaming in Restorative Justice", *The Red Feather Journal of Postmodern Criminology*, 8.

Rosenfeld, Richard, Joel Wallman and Robert Fornango (2005) "The Contribution of Ex-prisoners to Crime Rates", *Prisoner Reentry and Crime in America*, Washington (DC): The Urban Institute, pp. 80-104.

Ross, Jeffrey Ian and Stephen C. Richards (2003) *Convict Criminology*, Belmont (CA): Wadsworth.

Sentencing Project (2014) *Fewer Prisoners, Less Crime*, Washington (DC).

Tangney, June. P., Jeffrey Stuewig, Debra Mashek and Mark Hastings (2011a) "Assessing Jail Inmates' Proneness to Shame and Guilt: Feeling Bad About the Behavior or the Self?", *Criminal Justice and Behavior*, 38(7).

Tangney, June, P., Jeffrey Stuewig and Logaina Hafez (2011b) "Shame, Guilt and Remorse: Implications for Offender Populations", *Journal of Forensic Psychiatry & Psychology*, 22(5): 706-723

Terry, Charles M. (2003) *The Fellas*, Belmont (CA): Wadsworth.

Travis, Jeremy (2005) *But They All Come Back: Facing the Challenges of Prisoner Reentry*, Washington (DC): The Urban Institute.

Van Stokkom, Bas (2002) "Moral Emotions in Restorative Justice: Managing Shame, Designing Empathy", *Theoretical Criminology*, 6(3): 339-360.

Wacquant, Loïc (2009) *Punishing the Poor: The Neoliberal Government of Social Insecurity*, Durham: Duke University Press.

Welsh, Wayne N. and Gary Zajac (2004) "A Census of Prison-based Drug Treatment Programs: Implications for Programming, Policy, and Evaluation", *Crime & Delinquency*, 50(1): 108-133.

Western, Bruce (2006) *Punishment and Inequality in America,* New York: Russell Sage Foundation.

Wexler, Henry. K., Gerald Melnick, Lois Lowe and Jean Peters (1999) "Three-year Reincarceration Outcomes for Amity In-prison Therapeutic Community and Aftercare in California", *The Prison Journal,* 79(3): 321-336.

Zimmerman, Jack and Virgina Coyle (1996) *The Way of Council*, Putney (VT): Bramble Books.

ABOUT THE AUTHOR

Alan Mobley is an Assistant Professor of Criminal Justice and Public Affairs at San Diego State University. His research and writing builds upon his many years of direct involvement with the criminal justice system. Dr. Mobley teaches courses emphasizing perspective-taking, social justice and mindfulness practices. He credits his own prison experience as transformative in his life.

RESPONSE

Pains of Imprisonment, Everyday Deprivation and the Meanings of Post-Prison
Kevin Walby

Prisons and jails abolish our sense of our selves, through loss of autonomy, lack of material possessions, loss of say over sexual and personal relationships, reduced personal security, and forced racialization. Today's prisons and jails force people to pick sides, assault other sides, which is equally an assault on the self. These are the pains of imprisonment. They are real and lasting. The contributions found in this iteration of the *Journal of Prisoners on Prisons* (JPP) make it clear that these pains continue to be felt on the inside and post-prison as well.

Anonymous reflects on the devastating consequences of solitary confinement. His account of isolation and dispossession is chilling. Michael Johnson Jr. provides insight into sexualized prison violence and the issue of male rape. His story shows how unsettling and distressing such a brief violent encounter can be. Next, Robert Shoemaker, Brandon Willis and Angela Bryant consider the importance of education in prisons. Perhaps most worrying is that opportunities for education in prisons continue to dry up. Next, Daniel Luff and Greg Newbold raise questions about the culture of risk assessment in prisons and whether risk assessments do more harm than good. Exploring the vantage point of convict criminology, Alan Mobley demonstrates that shame built-up as a result of the pains of imprisonment can be immobilizing and upsetting. All the pieces in this issue of the *JPP* provide insight into the pains of imprisonment.

Prison agencies, including Canadian ones, tell us all these pains are offset by programing or a focus on rehabilitation. However, recent and significant changes at the federal level in Canada suggest otherwise. Since the contributors focused on the United States and other countries, I will provide context by focusing on Canada. Major changes federally in the Canadian context include rapid population growth. There are new precedents in all regions, such as double bunking in cells designed for single occupancy. In the Prairie region, fights and sexual assaults are up 60 percent. There are now more murders, more lockdowns, self-harm, and more administrative segregation, as well as double bunking in segregation in our federal penitentiaries. Prisoners and their advocates, but also guards have made complaints. All of this is according to the

Office of the Correctional Investigator (OCI) of Canada's annual report for 2012-2013.

This is a cycle of abuse. It starts with the pains of imprisonment that the authors in the *JPP* examine so clearly. The abuse is amplified by population growth and poor conditions. It is followed by segregation as punishment and segregation as means to manage prison populations. More use of segregation to manage this cycle means more abuse. It is almost as if the Government of Canada led by Conservative Prime Minister Stephen Harper thinks segregation is the solution to Canada's prison problems. We also see over-reliance on segregation to manage mental health issues, a disproportionate number of suicides in segregation, and a disproportionate number of First Nations men and women in segregation.

In Canada, we are witnessing exceptional change toward the conservative delusion of total segregation. What is happening in Canada's carceral state today will for certain inflame the pains of imprisonment tomorrow. As bad as that sounds, provincial jails are as bad or worse. Scholars in mainstream journals and in the *JPP* too over the years have tended to zero in on prisons rather than jails. The pains of being jailed certainly are long-term since some people do more time total in jail than in prison, where they are often moved around more frequently. People never know who they are in a cell with and staff hardly know either. Half or more of those held in jails are simply awaiting trial. This is the remand crisis. In some jurisdictions 85 percent of people in jail are waiting on the courts. There are class-dimensions, of course. Those in remand are often the subset of the presumed innocent who cannot afford to pay bail. And jails are becoming more chaotic in Canada as a result of several dozen changes to criminal law recently rolled out by Harper's Conservatives, sometimes at the request of their provincial counterparts.

These are big problems that seem to be getting worse in Canada. However, as the authors in this issue of the *JPP* point out, sometimes the mundane hurts more post-prison. Everyday deprivation is what many prisoners say hurts the most. In prison and jail you have no say over any thing. For people on the outside, when you wake-up you have a say over when to turn the lights on, you know where the light switch is, you have a say over which lights to turn on, where to step. Your place in the world is full of things and you have a say over them, how you will move down the hall, what room you go to next. Your relationship with the world around you is not a problem. But in prison and jail, it is made a problem by guards, administrators and other prisoners. I was trying to think of the common theme of all the *JPP* writings about the pains of imprisonment. One underlying feature is this: in prison and jail, you are deprived the fundamental good to have a say over the mundane aspects of life. Your relationship with things, with the walls around you, where you are standing – you have little say over any of it. As Anonymous puts it in this issue, you "can make no choices for yourself". Light switches on walls, how to move down a hallway, these are taken for granted outside. But when you cannot reach out and touch them, be in control of your self, your body and relationship to the world, it collapses you. Everyday deprivation. It is as lasting in its effects as the most bloody violence. So when people get out and we talk about pains of re-entry, these simple things can become overwhelming.

The exceptional. The mundane. The total range of pain that imprisonment causes. If we want to understand imprisonment we must map out the exceptional changes and trends, include accounts of the jail, and not overlook the little things that make prisons and jails make so little sense. The damaging effects of imprisonment will only be exacerbated by big changes we are seeing in Canada's carceral state. The articles that make up this volume of the *JPP* are courageous in tackling these issues that at times seem incomprehensible.

The other meaning of post-prison, of course, is making a world where we do not do this to one another anymore. The carceral state in Canada, in the United States, everywhere, is abusive. We must then try to commit to abolishing all organizations that attempt to abolish our sense of our selves.

PRISONERS' STRUGGLES

The John Howard Society of Ontario:
Effective, Just and Humane Responses to Crime
and its Causes for Over 85 Years
JHSO

> Those gentlemen who, when they are told of the misery which our prisoners suffer, content themselves with saying 'let them take care to keep out...', forget the vicissitudes of human affairs; the unexpected changes to which men are liable; and that those whose circumstances are affluent, may in time be reduced to indigence, and become debtors and prisoners.
>
> – John Howard (1777), page 23.

The John Howard Society is a charitable organization with lengthy roots in Ontario. The organization's namesake, John Howard, was a remarkable individual and his legacy guides the work that the John Howard Society continues to undertake today.

John Howard was an 18th century Englishman who was captured by the French while sailing from England to Spain. He subsequently spent five years in French dungeons before returning to England as part of a prisoner exchange. Eventually, he was made the Sheriff of Bedford, a post that included among its duties, the task of inspecting local prisons. Few sheriffs actually bothered to carry-out these duties, but John Howard was different. Shocked by the corruption, stench, filth, starvation and disease he saw in the jails, he dedicated his life to improving prison conditions throughout England, Wales and continental Europe. His famous report, *On the State of Prisons in England and Wales* led to legislation against the more obvious brutalities of the system, and slowly moved public opinion to favour more humane prison conditions.

In Ontario, the John Howard Society traces its roots back to classes taught in Toronto's Don Jail in the late 1800s. In a more formal way, the organization was founded in 1929 by Brigadier General Draper, then the Chief of Police in Toronto. Draper recognized the futility in much of the work being done by police, trying to solve crimes and apprehend wrongdoers, when prisoners who were being released from jail were thrust into circumstances of unemployment, isolation and poverty – circumstances that escalate rather than decrease the chances of re-offending.

Since 1929, the John Howard Society of Ontario (JHSO) has grown to include 19 local John Howard Society offices which serve communities all across our province, and advance our collective mission, *"Effective, just and humane responses to crime and its causes"*. Today, these local offices provide a variety of direct services to Ontarians and their families who have become, or are at risk of becoming, involved with the criminal justice system. The local offices provide services in a broad continuum of care from prevention programming to at-risk youth, institutional services and in-reach to prisoners, and reintegration support to those returning to the community after incarceration. John Howard Society clients have access to case management, individual counselling, addictions and mental health counselling, anger management counselling, employment services, housing, and other services either at the local John Howard Society office or through referral to other organizations.

In 2003, JHSO established its Centre of Research, Policy & Program Development (the Centre) to contribute to the evidence-based literature in the criminal and social justice fields, to inform policy discourse and to engage in rigorous program evaluation. The Centre's research, policy, and public education efforts are strategized to reflect and to further the mission of the provincial Society.

A key aspect of JHSO's mission is to promote the fair and humane treatment of all incarcerated persons and to seek to ensure that all forms of detention and imprisonment comply with relevant legal and human rights standards. Through the provision of institutional and reintegration services to both federal and provincial institutions in Ontario, the John Howard Society strives to ensure that individual prisoners' needs are being met, and that they are receiving supports and referrals that will help facilitate a successful transition back to the community (for those who are being released). Through the work of the Centre at JHSO, the Society both studies and profiles systemic issues in corrections and the social and criminal justice realm, in an effort to effect evidence-based and humane change.

Some of JHSO's key correctional policy priorities in recent years include high remand rates, prison overcrowding and bail in Ontario. Persons "on remand" are individuals being held in provincial custody awaiting bail, trial, or sentencing. The majority of the remand population is presumed to be legally innocent. Since the 1990s, fewer persons charged with criminal offences have been granted bail and have been detained in increasingly crowded, maximum-security detention centres until their charge is disposed of. In Ontario, approximately two-thirds of prisoners in our provincial institutions are those on remand – around 5000 persons on any given day (MCSCS 2013). In addition, approximately 70 percent of those on remand in Ontario are detained for non-violent charges (Porter and Calverley, 2011). Even short remand stays can be profoundly disruptive to a person's life.

JHSO has undertaken numerous studies, reports and submissions on the issue of remand, and most recently released a report entitled, *Reasonable Bail?* which found that bail in Ontario has drifted far from its legislated purpose, resulting more people detained pre-trial, as well as the erosion of the presumption of innocence and the guaranteed right to reasonable bail. Indeed, fewer people are being released on bail, less quickly, and with more bail conditions, during a time of historically low crime rates. Our provincial jails are crowded and at capacity; prisoners sleep two to three to a cell designed for one, at times on a mattress on the floor. While improving timely and broader access to bail will not solve all of the issues associated with high remand populations and crowding, it would make a significant impact.

Another solution to overcrowding in Ontario's provincial institutions that JHSO calls for is the re-invigoration and expansion of the use of community releases for sentenced prisoners. There has been a significant reduction in provincial parole and the use of conditional release programs in Ontario in recent decades. Additionally, as part of the reforms of the mid-late 1990s, the Ontario government eliminated halfway house and transitional housing programs for provincial prisoners, which has directly impacted the amount of transitional support available to reintegrating provincial prisoners (JHSO *et al.*, 2006). As our research has demonstrated, individuals who are justice-involved or are recently released from prison face a confluence of barriers upon re-entering society and need numerous support services. JHSO supports increasing the use of community-based sanctions, gradual release and prevention-focused programs, which reliably reduce rates of crime and victimization.

JHSO is uniquely positioned to have meaningful impacts on both our clients' lives through the services offered by local offices and on broader issues in Ontario. The organization's frontline expertise and connection to persons who have been in conflict with the law is critical to identifying current and emerging issues in our sector, which could necessitate a provincial JHSO response. Conversely, the research, policy and program evaluation work undertaken by the Centre ensures that the programs offered by the local John Howard Societies are evidence-led and impactful, and that challenges facing justice-involved persons in Ontario are being meaningfully documented and disseminated. The work of JHSO has certainly expanded since its formal inception in 1929, consistent with the evolving literature on social determinants of crime and successful responses to crime, but the organization remains committed to the values and vision espoused by John Howard many years ago.

REFERENCES

Howard, John (1777) *On the State of Prisons in England and Wales*, Warrington: William Eyres.

John Howard Society of Ontario (2013) *Reasonable Bail?*, Toronto. Retrieved from: <http://johnhoward.on.ca/pdfs/JHSO%20Reasonable%20Bail%20report%20final.pdf>.

John Howard Society of Ontario, Stephen Gaetz and Bill O'Grady (2006) *The Missing Link: Discharge Planning, Incarceration and Homelessness,* Toronto. Retrieved from:<http://johnhoward.on.ca/pdfs/The%20Missing%20Link%20%20Aug%202007.pdf>.

Ministry of Community Safety and Correctional Services (2013) *Daily Population Count Record – Adult*, Toronto – January 1.

Porter, Lindsay and Donna Calverley (2011) "Trends in the Use of Remand in Canada", *Juristat.*

COVER ART

Ronnie Goodman is a 54-year-old self-taught artist. He writes: I am sad to say I spent most of my life in and out of prisons battling drug addiction and struggling to find my own voice and way to a meaningful life. A twisted act of fate brought me to San Quentin State Prison on a ten-year term for burglary in 2003. There I signed up for the San Quentin Art Programs and the running club – that was the start of my new existence in life. I became a prolific artist and a long-distance runner, touched by the master artists and coaches who were my teachers and mentors. I was transformed into an artist and athlete, and not a prisoner. In 2010, I was released into society and into the despair of homelessness. However, a new life came to emerge through my running and creativity. My redemption: to contribute to raising the awareness of our social ills and to give back through my art and my running. I contribute by telling my story and donating my art – I recently donated a piece to the San Francisco Marathon as a fundraiser for Hospitality House, a homeless advocacy non-profit. My work and media stories about me can be viewed at http://www.ronniegoodman.com.

Front Cover: "The Boxer"
                 2009, linocut print on paper
                 Ronnie Goodman

"The Boxer" is a composition that I created at San Quentin Prison. I drew it from life – I saw something special there – a guy hitting a bag. While I was watching him I felt something. Perhaps it could be a metaphor for battling your demons, as many of us did in that place.

Back Cover: "Man at Work"
                 2014, linocut print on paper
                 Ronnie Goodman

"Man at Work" is inspired by a homeless man that I saw collecting two huge bags of bottles and cans making his way to the recycling centre. Our society looks down on people who do recycling, calling them "unsavoury characters". I tried to bring a different perspective – these are human beings, coming in early in the morning and doing their work. Just simple everyday life, but you never know why people's circumstances are the way they are.

www.ingramcontent.com/pod-product-compliance
Lightning Source LLC
Chambersburg PA
CBHW071233290326
41931CB00037B/2844